PRIESTESS
YOUR PLATE

My soul spirit being was searching to be heard, be understood in regard to nourishment. Half a lifetime of trying to fit in a square box of how 'I was to BE' or should be! How to feed your kids, family, how to feel, look and be happy. That all changed the moment I yarned to Tracey Pattison. Each session was a Returning—a coming home to my soul—spirit and connection to my Ancestors, culture and remembering and activation of a natural way of being. Therefore, my journey then became about me returning to a natural state of being and not to Fit in to a White privilege society that hijacked my Cultural way of life. To live and BE nourished from Mother and the Elements. Growing my food, respecting the local produce and food of the Water to nourish and sustain me. To allow my body rest and to practice what my Ancestors taught me: 'Take only what you Need.' From a deep part of my soul spirit, Tracey, the Ancestors and I honour you.
Annabelle Sharman, founder of A Sharman HOPE Healing

There's a vibration that comes from young children when they wholeheartedly delight in something – a deep hum, a gentle closing of the eyes, and, in my family, a little bum wiggle. *Priestess Your Plate* is like a big, delicious hug from your ancestors welcoming you home and thanking you for choosing to nourish yourself. There are gloriously simple, seasonal recipe pairings that are free from BS about superfoods and food fads. Tracey humbly takes us through her own 25-year experience of cooking and writing through the lens of diet culture. As Tracey says of food patriarchy, you'd have to be a mystical flying unicorn to have escaped it completely. Tracey reminds us that food and how we prepare and consume it, is an entire compassion practice for the self, for the earth, our ancestral traumas and the next generation for whom we pass all of this down to.
Dr Erin Bowe, Clinical Psychologist and author of *More Than a Healthy Baby: Finding Strength and Growth After Birth Trauma*

Welcome to the future of food and cooking. There's no question that when any activity becomes a spiritual practice it completely transforms the experience. The pages of this book are like a big warm hug, with incredible recipes and sacred food practices to boot. Your spiritual relationship to food begins NOW, in the most delicious of ways.
Ellie Swift, Mindset and Marketing Coach & Creator of the Swift Marketing Method®

Within the pages Mother Earth has spoken and Tracey has beautifully channeled what she desires All of us to hear. *Priestess Your Plate* is an offering to reconnect with ourselves and all that we have lost, allowing

us to deepen into our own food sovereignty. To reclaim our own food stories, by having a greater understanding of the cycles of Mother Earth and of ourselves. Allowing us to walk and invoke a sacred connection to kitchen craft. *Priestess Your Plate* initiates a deeper conservation with the sacredness of food, our wisdom and the magic of Mother Earth, giving womxn permission to change their food stories and live a more aligned life to Mother Earth and the ancient wisdom of our soul.
Larina Tiffen, founder of Priestess Lilly and Miss Lillys

Priestess Your Plate takes you on a beautiful journey that reconnects your soul, feeds and nurtures the Goddess within. Tracey Pattison invites you to re-energise, re-connect and re-member ancestral wisdom; to lean into your body and your intuition, while honouring the seasons, our stories and Mother Earth. Tracey creates space in the pages that guides you to really embrace the sacredness and rituals of food. She brings a wealth of knowledge and inner wisdom together to guide you as part of your priestess journey.
Nikki Tegg, creatrix of The Creative Goddess, author of *Goddess Rising: Soulful connection to empower and unleash your inner Goddess to rise above and see beyond*

Tracey Pattison is the modern food priestess who will help you to reclaim and remember your connection with Mother Earth and the healing gifts She is always offering to you. By reading Priestess Your Plate, you are able to reignite a passion for intentional and intuitive living in a simple and sacred way. This is an initiation into activating your inner goddess by creating an embodied practice filled with true nourishment of the mind, body and spirit. Thank you, Tracey for your wisdom, heart and your innate ability to nurture and heal through your words and through food, the Earth's Gifts.
Jacqueline Teej, wellness coach, inspirational speaker and author of *Master of One: A Soulmap for Conscious Living*

Tracey invites you into a sacred food revolution with *Priestess Your Plate*. A revolution that needs to happen in order to break away from patriarchal systems and structures that have stripped our connection to Mother Earth, and the Divine Mother's guidance within us when it comes to nourishing ourselves, cooking and food culture. *Priestess Your Plate* for me has been a compelling call to connect more deeply with my own ancestral food roots and to say yes to self-nourishment and empowerment through sacred devotion to my food and the Earth and Her seasons. Tracey is truly in service to you and the Goddess with deep reverence,

humility and joy as she takes you on a rich journey through the seasons of the Earth, guiding Goddesses, plant foods, seasonal recipes and other sacred supports so that you may then cultivate your own sovereign and intentional food practice. Within these pages is a complete and expansive modality for self-nourishment, devotional practice and the ingredients to change food culture for the better.
Lisa Kotz, Life and Self-Sovereignty Coach, founder of Inside the Prism

Priestess Your Plate is the homecoming to yourself you've been waiting for. As practical as it is wise, this book will give you the ultimate gift: the power to lead yourself to connect with who you are, how your body feels, and how to nourish yourself with food throughout every season and self-evolution to come. If you identify as intuitive—or even have the slightest inkling of your own intuition—the wisdom with these pages is here to activate your inner wisdom to whole new depths. The impact of Tracey's work and words is immediate and lasting. Once you pick up this book, you'll never want to put it down.
Miish Grixti, Copywriter and Launch Strategist at MiishGrixti.com

Since the birth of my three children, which coincided with my own personal spiritual awakening journey, I've felt lost in the kitchen. I've been able to feel fully empowered in my intuition in all areas of my life, except with food. I was always seeking, never satisfied, and felt disconnected. I've tried every fad. None have worked. Priestess Your Plate has given voice to this emptiness, and a pathway home. Tracey's energy, and love for food oozes from the pages of *Priestess Your Plate*. This is more than a cookbook, more than a food philosophy. It's a reclamation. The final piece of the spiritual awakening puzzle. A return home.
Shunanda Scott, angel medium, author of *The New Angel Messages*

Priestess Your Plate is the sacred work of art we need to connect us back to the Great Mother and the ever-flowing beautiful food she provides. It is a potent reminder of the integral relationship we must cultivate and preserve between ourselves and the bounties of the earth. Each page feels like an invitation into the magic of sensory delight—taste, scent and pleasure interwoven with grounded, feet-on-the-earth wisdom and brilliant storytelling. Reading through Tracey's words feels like being welcomed with open arms into a deeper and more delicious interaction with the foods we choose to eat and the rituals that can accompany and amplify each experience, taking you on a safe exploration into the world of true nourishment on all levels. *Priestess Your*

Plate is an intersection of spirituality, social awareness, seasonality and sass. It's an empowering catalyst for our awakening, or perhaps our re-learning, of our love of food, its origins and the reverence we can bring to it all. This book is going to be plucked with delight from home bookshelves across the world and be passed down through generations as we all prepare the dishes she's intuitively created, all the while with an elevated sense of devotion.
Sammie Fleming, Women's Coach, Workshop
and Women's Circle Facilitator

Priestess Your Plate is the book I needed to reignite my passion for food and cooking. It has brought back so many childhood memories around food and has reminded me how much I love to cook and entertain. I feel inspired to experiment in the kitchen and use food as a way to connect more deeply with myself, my ancestors and Mother Earth. I now see food—from selecting it, to cooking it, to eating it—as part of my spiritual practice and I can't wait to create my own rituals.
Emilie Gomez, Business Systems Strategist

Tracey Pattison has delivered a new way for womxn to come into connection with their body, their food and their soul. Guided by Tracey's deep wisdom of the vibration of food, her soul level love of womxn and nestled in the bosom of the Goddess, Priestess Your Plate feels like a homecoming for womxn. It is time for old beliefs and conditions about food and what it means to be a womxn to be dissolved and this book and Tracey's love and guidance feels like home.
Maree Eddings, creatrix of The Influential Womxn Movement

Witnessing the unfolding of Priestess Your Plate and the devotion and expression of Tracey herself has been an absolute joy. Tracey truly is THE Food Priestess! Tracey's passion for food and nourishment has enhanced the way I intuitively make magick in the kitchen and the way I revere nature's bounty. I love food and expressing myself as a kitchen witch. Some of my greatest memories include food in the cast of characters. Seasonal eating is one way to honour Mother Earth, and Tracey has much wisdom to share within these pages. With Tracey's guidance and lovingly crafted recipes, I am drawn deeper into flowing with and eating mindfully with the seasons. Tracey reminds us of the love and medicine food provides and the ancestral connection we have to food. I hope you too discover the sacredness of food and nourishment with Tracey as your guide.
Sharyn Holmes, CEO - Formidable Voices, Leadership Coach & Anti-Oppression Consultant, author of *Becoming Gutsy and Formidable*

PRIESTESS YOUR PLATE

seasonal FOOD and GODDESS initiations

TRACEY PATTISON

Copyright © 2021 Tracey Pattison
First published by the kind press, 2021

All rights reserved. No part of this book may be reproduced, stored in a retrieval system or transmitted in any form or by any means, electronic, mechanical photocopying, recording, or otherwise, without written permission from the author and publisher.

This publication contains the opinions and ideas of its author. It is intended to provide helpful and informative material on the subjects addressed in the publication. While the publisher and author have used their best efforts in preparing this book, the material in this book is of the nature of general comment only. It is sold with the understanding that the author and publisher are not engaged in rendering advice or any other kind of personal professional service in the book. In the event that you use any of the information in this book for yourself, the author and the publisher assume no responsibility for your actions.

Cover, illustrations and internal design by Nada Backovic
Edited by Alexandra McManus

Cataloguing-in-Publication entry is available from the National Library Australia.

ISBN 978-0-6488706-1-6
ISBN 978-0-6488706-2-3 (ebook)

To my husband and our two children, your unconditional love and acceptance is my constant drive and inspiration to be all that I can be, for you.

Mother Earth, thank you for holding me, without question, daily.

Acknowledgment to Country Australia

I acknowledge the Traditional Owners of the country on which I have created this piece of sacred work, where we live, work and where our feet connect with Mother Earth daily, the Gadigal people of the Eora nation, and recognise their continuing connection to the land, the sky, the waterways and culture. I pay my respects to their Elders past, present and emerging and acknowledge sovereignty of the land, sky and waterways has never been ceded. Australia's First Nation People are, have been, and always will be the true guardians. I ask that you now take time to research the lands on which you reside on and acknowledge who the traditional owners are.

Cultural Acknowledgment

My personal ancestry is Celtic and Slavic and as such you will find that I reference Goddesses from these cultures when spoken of in depth as I personally work with their energies heavily.

I want to honour and acknowledge here that the Goddesses that came forward to be in energetic alignment with the foods chosen through the initiations are from various different cultural backgrounds and they chose to step forward in allyship. While there are many cultures represented here, I do acknowledge that not all are given available space within this book. If your culture hasn't been represented, please take some time to explore them for yourself.

Family and Ancestry

I acknowledge and honour the sacred masculine in my husband and our son, and the sacred feminine within our daughter. I give great gratitude to both the red thread and white thread on both the Celtic and Slavic lines of my family's ancestral trees and the Scottish and Canadian ancestral lines of my husband.

WITHIN THESE SACRED PAGES

A Welcome Message	1
Note to Reader	3
Devotional Vow with Mother Earth	7
Your Invitation to Commune	9
Self-Activation for Priestess Your Plate	10

PART one THIS JOURNEY	13
About Priestess Your Plate	**15**
Insight of My Priestess Path	**23**
Priestess, The Goddess and Seasonal Food	**41**
You as Your Own Sacred Leader, as Priestess	**44**

PART two A DELICIOUS BECOMING	47
The Patriarchal Plate	**49**
Cycles of Self and Seasons of Mother Earth	**64**
Food Sacredness: Selecting, Cooking and Eating as Spiritual Practice	**70**
Selecting Food as Spiritual Practice	**73**
Cooking Food as Spiritual Practice	**75**
Eating as Spiritual Practice	**77**
Heart-Mapping Your Journey	**80**

PART three SEASONAL FOOD AND GODDESS INITIATIONS	85
Spring Food and Goddess Initiations	**93**
First Month Spring Rising	**97**
Asparagus and Goddess Vesta	99
Quick Roasted Asparagus Tart	102
Pink Grapefruit and Goddess Inanna	103
Vanilla Simmered Pink Grapefruit	106
Second Month Spring Surrender	**107**
Blood Orange and Goddess Athena	109

One-Bowl Blood Orange Teacake	111
New Potatoes and Goddess Diana	112
Sautéed New Potatoes with Spring Goddess Dressing	115
Third Month Spring Emerging	**116**
Pineapple and Goddess Pele	117
Chargrilled Pineapple and Mint Limes	120
Peas and Goddess Persephone	121
Steamed Pea and Lentil Toss	124
Summer Food and Goddess Initiations	**127**
First Month Summer Rising	**131**
Peach and Goddess Kuan Yin	132
Blanched Peach with Oolong Tea Syrup	135
Tomato and Goddess Abundantia	136
Braised Tomatoes for Simple Pasta	139
Second Month Summer Surrender	**140**
Eggplant and Goddess Nammu	141
Barbecued Marinated Eggplant and Smashed Hummus	144
Mango and Goddess Sol	145
Macerated Mango and Caramelised Macadamia	148
Third Month Summer Emerging	**149**
Blueberry and Goddess Artemis	150
Raw Blueberry Mousse	152
Mushroom and Goddess Aine	153
Stir-Fry Ginger Mushrooms with Udon	156
Autumn Food and Goddess Initiations	**159**
First Month Autumn Rising	**163**
Figs and Goddess Aphrodite	164
Figs with Saffron and Toasted Pistachio Crumb	167
Leek and Goddess Freya	168
Poached Leeks with Mustard Dressing	170
Second Month Autumn Surrender	**171**
Broccoli and Goddess Rhiannon	172
Grilled Broccoli and Quinoa Salad	175

Green Cabbage and Goddesses the Zorya	176
Pan-Fried Cabbage and Sage Gnocchi	179
Third Month Autumn Emerging	**180**
Apple and Goddess Pomona	182
Sweet Baked Apples with Pastry Top	184
Pear and Goddess Oshun	185
Preserved Pears	187
Winter Food and Goddess Initiations	**189**
First Month Winter Rising	**194**
Celeriac and Goddess Isis	195
Celeriac Soup with Dukkah Flatbreads	198
Sweet Potato and Goddess Hecate	199
Roasted Sweet Potatoes with Harissa Barley	202
Second Month Winter Surrender	**203**
Lemon and Goddess Frigga	205
Little Lemon Puddings	208
Beetroot and Goddess Kali Ma	209
Slow-Roasted Beetroot Curry	212
Third Month Winter Emerging	**213**
Rhubarb and Goddess Hel	215
Stewed Rhubarb Crumble	218
Dates and The Morrigan	219
Slow-Cooker Sticky Date Choc Cake	221
CLOSING CEREMONY	223
A Closing Vow	225
Priestess Your Plate Path Forward	226
Recipe Notes	228
Priestess Gratitude	229
Bibliography	230
About the Author	231
Food Index	234

A Welcome Message

WELCOME delicious one, welcome to *Priestess Your Plate*.

Welcome to food sacredness.

Welcome to selecting, cooking and eating
food as a joyful, spiritual practice.

Welcome back to where your divine,
sovereign needs are met.

Welcome to the release of food fear, food
privilege and food demonising.

Welcome back to you as your own
sacred leader, you as Priestess.

Welcome to our Great Goddess, Mother Earth
and Her daily unconditional love for us.

Welcome back home to a heart, mind, body and spirit that
feels alive, connected and nourished with seasonal food.

Welcome.

Note to Reader

I am honoured you've arrived here, at these pages of this book.

The calling.
Mother Earth has put a sacred call out for us to listen to, for us to rise higher into the fullness of who we truly are. A call to act in deep, authentic and compassionate love towards self with how we nourish our hearts, minds, bodies and spirits… and how we do this with food. To use food, cooking and eating as a sacred, spiritual practice—the ultimate act of self-loving care that we can give to ourselves first and then to others. To return to food sacredness—to the way it used to be many, many moons ago—to that time you may just remember, that time where our grandparents and great ancestors viewed and honoured food simply, humbly and for the deepest nourishment of self.

As a collective community we have been craving this, for years. This coming back home to the way things used to be, a simpler way. This craving, this need, has stemmed from the desire to step as far away as possible from the decades of food patriarchy which has led to our intuitive voice being overridden by others—media, government, celebrity and the multi trillion-dollar health and wellbeing industry.

Food is something so humble, such a basic need that's grown from Mother Earth Herself, that our grandparents or elder carers when we were growing up seemed so much more connected to. So how did food become such a commodity that has instilled the greatest amount of fear? And fear particularly directed at women-identifying too.

Mother Earth, the greatest Goddess of all, is asking you now to remember, and if you can't remember to spend some time getting to know this lost part, this knowledge that is a birthright.

This is the ask.
She is asking for you to return to Her, to return to the simplicity that is living within Her seasons, enjoying Her foods and invoking it all through sacred practice that is steeped in your cycles of self and your ancestry. This calling is for allyship. For you to connect deeper to Her. To feel Her love, Her embrace and Her nurturing power through food.

She wants to see you thrive. And She wants you to understand that what once worked in the past is no longer of service anymore. The change has begun. Have you felt this change? Have you found that you're questioning all that you once knew or felt comfortable with around food? Are you completely confused by all the mixed messages of food, diet culture and what 'healthy' really is? Are you beginning to see through the veil that food patriarchy has formed?

It's OK if you don't know the answers to all of this, yet... because we will journey further through these pages for you to discover it all. For you to discover that there is so much more to food than what we've been fed for so many years. That food should be the least fearful item in your life, that cooking can come from a place of passion and that you have all the wisdom you need, right inside of you, to nourish yourself wholly.

Her ask of me.
Mother Earth asked me directly, too, which is why it was time for me to write Priestess Your Plate. This was my call-to-action and something that I have long desired to write about, but divine timing has had me wait until this exact moment.

Welcome to **Priestess Your Plate.**
An invitation for you to reconnect with and understand your intuitive self through the sacred practice of food—selecting, cooking and eating in alignment with your cycles of self and Mother Earth's seasons for sovereign nourishment in heart, mind, body and spirit.

Welcome to the path of the Priestess, through food. Welcome to embodying the sacred feminine leadership energy that is the Priestess and infusing it into food under the delicious guiding cycles that are Mother Earth's seasons. The patriarchal plate has ended. It has well and truly served its course, and the pages of *Priestess Your Plate* and Her Seasonal Food and Goddess Initiations are here to be of the greatest service to you.

Welcome to no more food or body shaming.

Welcome to no more ingredient or food-lifestyle demonising.

Welcome to no more food privilege.

Welcome to the utter magick that you will discover as you journey through the initiations of each individual seasonal food item and their energetically matched Goddess. Welcome to learning how to honour your whole self, in heart, mind, body and spirit with food.

It's time.
It's time to reconnect to our own food truths; reclaim our own authentic food beliefs; to carry on the voice of our ancestral food storytelling; to open our hearts and hands to Mother Earth and Her environment and to live in alignment with our sovereign, Priestess selves.

Welcome, welcome to these sacred pages of *Priestess Your Plate* and to a reclamation of yourself through food sacredness.

Welcome home.

And so it is.
Tracey x

Devotional Vow with Mother Earth

You can take this vow along with me by simply speaking it internally or aloud.

I vow in heart, mind, body and spirit that I Am;
Consciously connected daily,
In devotional practice with,
And co-create all that I do,
With our Great Goddess, Mother Earth (Her).

I vow to be in alignment with Her seasons;
To blossom and be joyfully creating in spring,
To celebrate and be seen in summer,
To let go and be in grateful connection in autumn,
To surrender and be in gentle reflection in winter.

I vow to remember that;
I can cry, cleanse and be in flow like water,
I can burn, tame and ignite like fire,
I can be still, focused and decide like air,
And I can be grounded, build and give like Her.

I vow to honour my sovereign self, in
all aspects that She holds me;
As Priestess I channel wisdom between all realms,
As Goddess I embody feminine intuition,
As Witch I transform through magick,

*As Nature Child I commune with
animals, plants and all Her allies.*

*I vow that nourishment reciprocity is our foundation;
As I receive from Her, I give back to Her,
And So It Is,
That our interwoven cycles continue for all time.*

And so it is.

I am Tracey Pattison, Priestess to Mother Earth

Your Invitation to Commune

May we collectively nourish, share wisdom and commune further together.

Priestess Your Plate live
Head to www.traceypattison.com/pyp-book to see the list of free resources, events and sacred food ceremonies that I will be doing in correlation with this delicious book throughout the seasons.

Self-Activation for Priestess Your Plate

I welcome you to repeat out loud the following incantation to self-activate your inner wisdom, your intuitive self, so that the words written in this text connect deeply to your four energetic bodies—emotionally, mentally, physically and spiritually—to receive whole of self, sovereign nourishment.

Then seal its energy by writing your name at the start and then adding your signature and the date at the end.

I,  ,

open my heart, mind, body and spirit to the energetic connections between the words within this sacred text of Priestess Your Plate *to my own inner wisdom, reigniting my intuitive self.*

I call upon an intertwined Divine union between Mother Earth and myself.

May Her wisdom shared through Her food messengers' readings and the Goddesses provided within the pages of Priestess Your Plate *imprint in me the sacred connection to myself as leader, as Priestess, and to Her.*

I will stand in sovereignty, honouring at all times my personal cycles of self through the seasons of Mother Earth, knowing in heart, mind, body and spirit that I am an ever-changing, ever-expanding, ever-evolving, cyclic being throughout this spiral journey of life.

I am present, I am whole, I am ready.
The time for me is NOW.
And so it is.

_____

Signed

On this date,_____, of the month _____, in the year of _____.

PART *one*
THIS JOURNEY

About Priestess Your Plate

Why this book? Why now? Because living with any component of food fear or to live with any notion of food patriarchy is no longer an option if we are to walk on Mother Earth feeling nourished and connected. We belong; we are here to serve our purpose-driven lives and to view our whole selves with complete love and compassion. Because the time of giving over our personal power to follow an outside self, 'guru', teacher, healer, coach, influencer or guide just simply no longer works. And in doing so we become disconnected, lost and undernourished in heart, mind, body and spirit. Mother Earth is asking us to commune with, connect to and be nurtured by Her for our greatest good.

At this present time, human-produced environmental changes have Her traversing in a way that She's never experienced before. She will endure, just as she has always done throughout 'Herstory', but for us, we simply will not, and this is why She is calling us forward to energetically realign to the way that we did in the past. Way back when She was honoured and celebrated for Her seasons and what each of these seasons offered us in return. Where the sacred feminine was honoured through all cultures and through the energies of the Goddess while deeply held by the devoted Priestesses of the time. Where we sought refuge, replenishment and revitalisation through Her and by Her. Through Her seasons, Her elements and by the food grown by Her.

It's time to cultivate love, compassion and true authentic nourishment through food—how we select, cook and eat with sovereignty. This is a magickly humble journey that will reignite your inner wisdom, your intuitive self, and birth a new, joyful way of connecting with food.

You'll discover your unique and authentic self through food sacredness, working alongside Mother Earth's seasons, understanding your personal cycles of self and gaining added knowledge through the food messengers and their aligned Goddesses. The food messengers will give you a deeper understanding of their energetic wish for you and the Goddesses show just what a divine, multifaceted be-ing you are. It's a true 'becoming' of sorts, where you discover that you can easily, and quickly, become your own sacred leader.

A Sneak Peek of What You Can Expect

I'll take you on a journey through my own personal experiences with food sacredness, how I cook and personally eat, what I know to be true at this moment in time for myself and what She is asking for me to share with you. As I continue to deepen my work in the world as a Priestess to Mother Earth, I am also in constant learning and I am devoted to being in communion with, and nourished by, Her daily through the seasonal plant foods She nurtures for us to eat.

I simply LOVE food; I always have, and I always will. I've always felt a deep connection to food, its sacredness, and I have been passionate about learning and sharing as much as humanly possible about it my whole life. I simply love the pure magick it holds for us to tap into. In writing the words to this book I was able to dedicate time in each of the seasons to really infuse all that I could energetically while working alongside the Celtic and Slavic Goddesses of my ancestry. Spring was Goddess Brigid (sacred flame), summer was Goddess Mokosh (water and Earth Mother), autumn was Goddess Airmed (healing) and winter was Goddess Cerridwen (cauldron).

So please know that I have devotionally held you through each of these seasons with all of my energetic bodies too—in heart, mind, body and spirit—so that you can feel each season as the true, delicious experiences that they are and how they've been shared through my words.

Women, The Sacred Feminine, Priestess and Goddess

When I refer to women, Priestess or Goddess I am encompassing women, women-identifying beings or anyone who holds the energy of the sacred feminine within whether 'male' or 'female' (cisgendered) or gender fluid.

Mother Earth

I refer to Mother Earth as such, or as the great Goddess, Mother Earth or the Great Mother. Please understand with my cultural heritage that these terms are steeped in my ancestry but also know that the energy of Her is the same energy that is present through all of Her names throughout the world, some of which are Pachamama, Gaia, Great Mother, Earth Goddess, Country or more. Invoke Her name as it feels true for you based on your own cultural identity.

Seasons

The seasons are referenced throughout as the four 'main' commonly western-known seasons of spring, summer, autumn and winter. Again, as the eclectic, global community of readers that you are, hold true in your heart the season's energy that feels most true for you and where you reside geographically on Mother Earth, as they may expand, or contract given your geographic location and own cultural identity.

Plants-First Recipes

My recipes shared in these pages come to you as they come to me and how we enjoy them at home. That is, the recipes use ingredients directly sourced from Mother Earth herself, as purely as possible. I hold and stand energetically by my personal devotion to plants-first on every plate and so this is reflected in the recipes. But please note this is not a prescription for you to do the same. It's offered as an exploration or a starting point for mealtimes.

When I refer to 'food' throughout the book, I am wholeheartedly talking directly about all plant foods grown by Mother Earth, that are lovingly tended to by the dedicated growers, farmers and pickers to allow for them to come from Her to us every day. I wish for you to hold in whichever capacity you see fit for yourself what plants-first may (or may not) mean for you. Journey with this based on your culture, beliefs, morals and ethics and how your body feels when you eat.

Plants-first could mean some, all or none of the following to you but I feel it is worth sharing to spark some deeper explorations of self:

- Meals and dishes derived solely from plant foods with no meat, poultry, seafood or other animal-derived products added.

- Meals or dishes where plant foods are the most predominant feature with small amounts added of animal-derived products such as dairy or eggs.

- Meals or dishes where plant foods are the most predominant feature with small amounts added of meat, poultry, seafood and their animal-derived products.

Please also explore that as the seasons change, so too can the general day-to-day make up of your meals. Summer may invoke a 100% plants-first plate because lighter-feeling meals suit your energy best on the long, hot summer days and/or in wintertime you may find great soul comfort in slow-cooked meats along with your vegetables. In every which way possible, it is all OK as long as how you are choosing to eat whichever foods you desire always comes from a place that honours you most in the season you are in or the personal cycle of self you are journeying through.

I have added additional notes and ways you can add to each of these recipes too, offering you options to honour how it is that YOU desire to eat also.

Eating and Mealtimes

As individual be-ings we each walk on Mother Earth with such varied needs in how food plays a role in our energetic bodies, so please tune in to listen to yours. Like, *reallllly* listen. There's so much noise 'out there' and this is the easiest, most lost part of ourselves that I see when sitting in sacred space with clients.

For instance, there is no point forcing food in the mornings if you're simply not hungry or can't stomach it but feel the need to do so because of that time-old catchphrase, 'Breakfast is the most important meal of the day,' which, by the way, was thoroughly advocated worldwide by Dr John Harvey Kellogg when he went out to sell a newly invented breakfast cereal flake, no less. The phrase was written in a feature story about eating a 'lighter' meal at breakfast time in the company's related magazine, *Good Health*, in 1917. The writer, who was an employee of Dr Kellogg's company, Leena F. Cooper, B.S. happened to be in mentorship with Dr Kellogg at the time too.

I've personally never been able to eat breakfast on waking. Especially throughout my teen years it would make me feel physically sick and even more so now as I age I'm finding that my first 'meal' of the day tends to be around lunchtime. My husband and our little girl are completely different to me, they both wake up and eat a hearty meal straight away, whereas our son is much like me however he tends to eat closer to 8–9 am instead.

The reason I share this is so you can explore on your own, again, what suits you best. If you happen to have young children, be mindful that they may just be different to you and are not simply refusing certain foods at different times of the day to purely push your buttons.

For myself, the greatest gift I've realised with not only food, but everything, is that there is always choice and in true food sacredness there doesn't have to be an either/or option too, you can have both. What I mean by this is, and this is very true to me and my absolute love and devotion to all things potato, is that I desire to not choose an either/or option but instead choose both. So, for instance, if we were eating out somewhere I would be ordering the following: 'I'll take the pasta dish thanks with both the mash potatoes *and* fries on the side.'

You see I grew up in a household with a potato-loving Irish-born father, so we had a serving of potatoes with every meal. Butter chicken and roast spuds? *Well of course!* Beef tacos and fries? *Oh, Goddess yes!* And let's not forget everyone's all-time favourite, spaghetti bolognese and mash, *ya damn straight I'm having that!*

As you'll read further, when I share with you in greater depth about Food Patriarchy in Part two from page 49 onwards, if the way you eat—how, when, with what and the like—feels forced, fearful or you feel wrong or bad after not doing something that is being prescribed to you, then this is a clear sign of being coerced into an unaligned food requirement for self. When it's not food patriarchy, it should and will feel easy to you. Your energy body will feel alive and happy, and that you aren't missing out or have any sense of being deprived.

Checking Privilege

It goes without saying that as best as possible I've written this sacred book from a place of do no harm in terms of privilege. It must be heavily noted that I am a white woman, so I walk on Mother Earth instantly with so much more privilege than many.

Insight of My Priestess Path

Food has always been my guiding compass in the world. My one true constant throughout my day-to-day life as far back as my memory allows; throughout my twenty-five year business in food publishing and now in my sacred work as a modern practising priestess. It's fun to journey backwards through it all to see how all of the golden threads were woven to bring me to the present-day, to where you are now holding this book in your hands and reading Her words.

Come back in time with me now, and bear witness to a seasoning of fond early-childhood memories I have had with food. It will give you deep insight into why food is such a passion of mine, why it is literally in my DNA. My first conscious childhood memory is of food. I can tell you a story of food in every year of my life from that point on.

I am two years old, sitting in my highchair in the kitchen. The kitchen is red. There are bold red cabinets and a bench top, with red wallpaper lining the walls. It's the 1970s. There are three lamb chops in front of me and I'm loving banging them together, gnawing down on them and just watching my mum as she seems to glide across the kitchen in precision.

I know she is busy getting the rest of dinner ready and she's so happy doing it, singing to a record playing—most definitely *Hot August Night* by Neil Diamond—and glancing big smiles my way as I babble on with my lamb chops. I can still *sense* her happiness to this day through this memory.

I am six years old. I've just woken up. My nan lovingly yells at me, in that maternal Irish way, to go sit in her chair. It's placed right in front of the TV for perfect viewing. I'm excited, even though I can't express that, as again, it's winter and I have tonsillitis. I always get tonsillitis in the winter. It always happens around my birthday too. Nevertheless, I'm excited because I'm sitting in Nan's chair in front of the telly after just waking up. I'm also excited because it's just my Granda, Nan and me together at their house and I'm just about to receive the best breakfast *ever*.

It's a strawberry jam sandwich, on fluffy white bread, cut into triangles. *Yes!* A jam sandwich for breakfast.

I am seven years old. I've just arrived at Baba and Deda's house. It's Saturday, we always visit them first on a Saturday. There is one thing on my mind: those strawberry bushes in the front yard. On arriving, I do an inventory of my mum's conversation to Auntie's over the week and immediately know that no other grandchildren have visited... I'm the first one to arrive at their house for the week. I know what that means!

We are no longer than a few minutes inside and Baba hands me a little china teacup filled with sugar and pushes me back out the door to go pick the strawberries all the while saying, 'Darr-gi (darling), eat, eat, eat,' with the warmest, most loving voice you've ever heard. That one sentence of hers was a mantra my whole life, for all of us in the family actually: Darr-gi, eat, eat, eat. The absolute joy on her face when she saw the family eat her food was delightfully infectious and I delight in knowing I get that aspect from her. I run out to their front yard with the same level of excitement of Christmas morning when you reach the tree and see just how many gifts Santa has left for you. I gasp as I reach the bushes as I can see some little red jewels on there. They're perfect, and I thank the faeries for them.

'There are five! No, wait, underneath there's more. Yes, yes!'

I sit beside the bushes with my teacup of sugar and pick what feels like oceans of strawberries from the bushes. I sit on the grass eating and dipping them into the sugar as I go. I'm in heaven.

I am eight years old. I just got home from school for the day. Mum heads back downstairs to keep working as I throw my bag on the floor. Without waiting, I switch on the oven and grab the Date Loaf packet mix from the pantry. I gather all the extra ingredients, loaf pan and utensils and set myself up on the kitchen bench—everything perfectly laid out and in order—and then I begin. The director calls 'action' and I start with my cooking segment, being mindful to look up and talk into the camera as needed—without risking the quality of the cake—as I prepare it. I even take cooking questions from the 'live' imaginary audience members too. This weekly ritual lasts for a few years and the family is pretty happy as there is always a delicious slice of date loaf to enjoy with lashings of butter.

I have a lifetime of these memories of food, cooking and eating. At bare minimum, three per year that always stick out to me. There are so many more of these throughout my childhood, teen years and adult life. These food memories of such delicious happiness, such fun, such celebration. Growing up with food as the centrepiece of gatherings, of conversation, of shared wisdom and of love expressed. And expressed through both women and men on both sides of our families. But it wasn't until I had left home as an adult that I realised this wasn't the norm. I had reached the age of twenty-four believing that everyone grew up like this. Yeah, I know, first big foodie light-bulb moment there!

My Slavic family, my mum's side, were market farmers. Deda first started growing tomatoes on their land when they immigrated from Flensburg, Germany, where they had been waiting on UN territory to get a boat to Australia after being held captive in prison war camps that were called working farms. 'The land was so fertile,' he would always say. Perfect for tomato growing, but not before long he found that he was growing everything that he could in season to sell at the fresh produce markets. They had a cow, chickens and not much money so everything Baba made was 'made from scratch', a term now used as a marketing gimmick in the food world. She made butter, ricotta, filo pastry, pasta noodles for soup—everything. Even after retiring and moving to a smaller suburban house, Deda still had his hands in the soil growing vines. He nurtured those grapes with such devotion—along with an endless battle with the birds every single summer—and made wine with them. Enough wine to service the whole family for gatherings for the year. Some years, batches would explode in his carport area. Other years, the sugars created a seriously intoxicating alcohol level.

I was beyond devastated to find out that these vines, which were clippings he had carried with him from his homeland all those many years ago, were pulled out and discarded, along with the trash, after he and Baba had crossed their rainbow bridges.

It makes me cry even now while writing these words—what I would have given to have even just one of those vines to personally carry the heirloom legacy of his hands through to our children. The storytelling they would experience *while* tending to, looking at and eating those grapes today.

My Irish family, my dad's side, immigrated to Australia after my dad decided to take the ten pound boat ride on offer. Granda had been a chef in the Royal Merchant Navy. He was quiet, took ages to eat his meals and was devoted to Nan. She was a fierce, firm and deeply loving woman who always announced that she was from Belfast, Northern Ireland. A true matriarch.

Granda was the cook of the home and this is something, again, that I had always thought was obviously a common thing to happen in families—that both men and women cook for their families full-time. Sunday roast dinners, Irish stew, braises and baked desserts with scoops of vanilla ice cream were the specialty. But Granda's winter soup—ham hock and vegetable—that was *him*. Every year he would make a huge stockpot of the soup. And every year as we'd get the first bowls served up with a side of buttered boiled potatoes and dash of HP sauce for dipping in, we'd exclaim, 'Now that's a lovely drop!'

Both sets of my grandparents loved to cook and eat and celebrate with food. From this, my parents loved to cook, eat and celebrate with food. And so, it's with no surprise that my older sister and myself grew up loving food and do the same. Cook, eat, celebrate... on repeat. It's in our DNA. Loving the art of food preparation, entertaining, trying new things, cooking for our families and friends and exploring the world through food—we both have this passion. And from all of my childhood food love and experiences, laying a solid foundation for how food, cooking and eating can be a great source of deep connection and love for ourselves, others and our Great Mother Earth (more on this later), you can imagine my absolute pure and utter shock and excitement that I could make a career from food, and through a most artistic sense too.

A Delicious Career

What do you mean there is a career path through food creation, developing recipes and writing cookbooks? This blew my mind, the concept of being able to build a career that was based on all of my loves in life—food, cooking, eating, creating art, working with my hands and writing—and doing it all through the freedom of choosing how I would work, where I would work and for how many hours I would work. I grew up in a household where my mum ran her own business from home and I loved that so much as a child, so I had no fear of creating my own business as well. It always felt right, even logical to do and completely achievable that I could run my own business one day also.

I completed a food course in college with high distinctions. It was the first time in my whole schooling career where I realised that I was a practical, hands-on learner and that when I found a topic that I was head-over-heels passionate about that the learning became effortless. I still stand by this marker, even today, as it's my guiding compass for what mentors I will choose to work with year-on-year and what I lend my creative energy to. I won national recipe writing awards throughout this time and did as many hours of free work experience that I could with anyone who would have me. I had finally discovered what felt true to me. I just wanted to be on set and see those photographers in action, snapping away images of the food that I had created—and created with such precision, such care and so much love to the detail—honouring the food as it should be.

My unwavering passion and desire to learn, expand and get as much experience as possible in my industry was my internal fire and I worked my way through it all quite quickly, becoming the youngest food editor in the country on a magazine just a few years later.

I soon got itchy feet in Australia when I knew there were no more career avenues for me to explore, or industry greats to learn from as I had worked with and alongside them all.

So, I cashed in my frequent flyer points and got a one-way ticket to the United Kingdom (UK). London was everything I knew it would be; it fit me like an old favourite glove. I knew the streets so very well, even though I'd never walked them. The climate suited my temperament and the food publishing world felt expansive, a new threshold for me to cross, and I felt alive again. I was twenty-six years old.

I landed in London and finally felt free. Free from past relationships with men, free from the restraints of working in a small industry in Sydney, free to be an adult separate from all of my family and friends. I could be the adult I had longed for, a travelling, unchained, ever-expansive adult really living her life fully in the world. And then three months in, and without seeking it, I met the love of my life who I'm deliciously married to now, eighteen years later. We stayed in London for a while longer and I was able to work with so many rising food industry greats while there, such as Jamie Oliver, Nigella Lawson and Nigel Slater to name a few.

Itchy again to explore the world more, we moved to the United Arab Emirates (UAE) in the Middle East and lived in a very small local town on the border of Oman. It was eye opening, heart wrenching, hard and fun all at the same time. Again, I easily found my feet in food publishing there and wrote the weekend lift-out magazine food pages and worked with world-leading advertising agencies like Saatchi and Saatchi.

Two years on we decided to move again. This time we headed to Penang, Malaysia. On all accounts it was a rushed move and we both quickly regretted it after landing. A beautiful island with lovely, welcoming locals and incredible food, but the ex-pat community was unforgiving and after only a few months I headed back to Sydney, while my husband finished that first half-year mark in his job and then joined me.

Landing back in Sydney, I stepped straight back into the throws of the food publishing world and was instantly booked out with clients. To be honest, I wasn't ready to come home full-time yet. I still felt I needed to be travelling and working my way across Europe, but Divine timing had brought me back for a reason. A reason that wouldn't be known until four months later.

Then I Broke

Just four months into being back in Sydney the devastating news that my dad had stage 4 bowel cancer landed. I then knew the reason why I had this strong feeling to be back home in Sydney when we were in Penang. This news felt surreal. *My dad. MY dad. How could this be? This simply could not be happening to us, to our family, to my dad.* He was my everything, we were two peas in a pod in personality. We could sit for hours in silence in each other's company and yet it would feel as though we had traversed all conversations. He was the one who prompted me to move overseas and leave Sydney behind for a while. He knew me better than I knew myself. And he still does now.

Dad's initial diagnosis was that he would only survive a few months. The absolute fear I felt at that time literally opened a vault within me of early childhood trauma that I had no recollection of happening when I was between the ages of two and four. I was experiencing horrific visions; would hear words being said to me and had endless nightmares of the recounts of the horrific things that happened to me. I seriously thought that I was beginning to lose my mind, and not to mention the rollercoaster of emotions I was feeling at witnessing my dad's journey with cancer treatments, and the effect that was having on my mum and our family unit. It was all too much to try and comprehend what was happening that I literally had no idea what to do.

I had never asked for help before in my life, up until that point, but I knew I needed to do something drastically, so I sought professional help. I had an incredible therapist who supported me in understanding that the brain can do wonders in trying to keep us 'safe' at times of immense trauma, and that my early childhood experiences had simply been locked away until that same level of fear arose again. And since Dad's diagnosis absolutely rocked me to my core, it was the key to unlock what had been trapped inside of me for so many years. I was coming into my thirty-first year.

Dad crossed his rainbow bridge one year later, and again, I understood the privilege it was to have a business where I could dedicate so much time to being with Dad through that year of immense treatments, the highs and lows of it all. Such a sacred time, what a blessing.

But as time progressed and we planted our roots in Sydney, I could really feel the energy of the industry shifting and my business itself change. It started to feel heavy, a feeling I'd never had in my career prior. It was unsettling and I simply tried to combat this feeling by stuffing it all down and working even harder. However, as our second born, our little girl, was welcomed Mother Earth-side, I knew in my bones that a shift had happened in the food publishing industry that I had always felt so deeply connected to. This shift was so great, and I began to understand the industry that I once knew had changed so drastically that it could, and would, never be the same again—no matter how hard I tried or worked. Those times of change in food publishing changed fast and I literally could no longer emotionally, mentally, physically or spiritually continue doing what I was doing. It no longer held the same morals and ethics that it once did when I first started my career.

I then began to realise that I was contributing to part of the problem. What I felt so internally against, I was actually contributing to, and this really played havoc on me. I was still creating for what I no longer believed in. Morals and ethics were dwindling in the industry and it went against every cell in my body, and my body was physically reacting to it too. This battle within myself went deep and dark and I really lost my way. The heaviness of grief at losing my dad, my soul mate, on top of it all didn't help either. I even lost the excitement to cook and eat. This was when I knew I needed to do something drastic, and fast. Never in my life or career had I felt this way with just an absolute numbness to food. I was living on caffeine all day, eating bowls after bowls of food at dinner, washed down with red wine and not sleeping well. Our home felt tight. I had an urge to just flee and I felt ridiculously uncomfortable being outside and around others.

My Personal Journey, the Dark Night of The Soul Came Knocking

I was ready to make any changes required at this point, I just didn't know what to do or how to do it. I had only ever known my business and the food publishing industry.

If I didn't have that, then what did I have? So, I said yes to something else. I said yes to something that I had no idea about or what it meant. I said yes to a course that was focused on women in business and based in spirituality.

Spirituality... (?) At thirty-nine years of age, I had no idea what this term meant. Was this religion? I didn't believe in organised religion. But I was so drawn to the words that were used to describe this course that I was willing to jump in and try it anyway. It was a course called Soulpreneurs. It was magickly crafted by Yvette Luciano, the first female mentor I had who wasn't involved in food and who was spiritual. A true Earth Angel who now resides in the heavens after crossing her rainbow bridge in early 2020.

This course was filled with women, something that I feared most—being surrounded by women I didn't know—and as I sat on the floor in our first in-person gathering at my first-ever women's circle (sweating with fear), I felt like I was home. There was soft music playing, candles lit everywhere and this woman, Yvette, sitting cross-legged on the floor in front of me with the biggest, warmest and most welcoming smile I'd ever seen. I can't remember the words she spoke, but I remember how she made me feel. It felt so foreign to me to feel this kind of connection with another woman, to feel so comfortable in her presence, but it felt so right. It felt as though I had taken the deepest breath ever and that I would be forever changed.

And I was.

The Awakening of Me Started

It was an exhilarating ride, this spiritual journey that then unfolded as the Soulpreneurs community gathered deeply and connected over everything from family life, to business life and every other facet of who we were as individuals and as a collective. And *all* of the in-betweens. I discovered some seriously 'lost' magickal powers I had within me, like sensing other people's energy fields, being able to 'see' and 'know' what their bodies required from food and having a wickedly addictive connection to Mother Earth, all her sentient beings and elemental worlds. I astral travelled in my sleep, had rememberings from past lives (some horrific, some so blessed) and every step of the way I just kept feeling I was becoming so much more of who I truly was as a person, at a soul level. And I loved it.

Officially hooked on *all* things spiritual, I bought oracle decks, used incense and essential oils, read any book I could find on the subject and explored all areas to see what felt good and what didn't land fully or felt was my truth. I was just as excited to learn again as I had been when I was in college years prior. This feeling of learning with such passion again, finding a love for spirituality that matched my love of all things food. *Could there really be another love in my life that wasn't food?* What a revelation that was.

This spiritual exploration began to show me why I had felt so different to other people my whole life. Why I didn't like being in big crowds, why I'd rather observe than take part, why I couldn't do all of the 'inside the box' stuff that so many people felt comfortable doing. I felt this urge that I had something greater I needed to do out in the world, I just didn't know what it was, so I began to explore. I limited myself to only working with certain people in my industry. I thought if I surrounded myself with more aligned people in food publishing that would work, but it didn't. Perhaps if I stopped writing cookbooks for others and wrote one myself that would work, so I approached publishers with my ideas, and they weren't interested. So, I thought I'd self-publish my own cookbook. But that didn't work either. I felt again that it was all getting too heavy, and fast. Nothing worked. It was dead end after dead end.

I journalled. I prayed. I spoke to Mother Earth and there was nothing—no response, no information coming through, no insight, even my dad had stopped visiting me… or so I thought. I immersed myself in an incredible business-focused mastermind to see If I could shift that way. Perhaps I had become too spiritual *(like that's a thing, or even possible!)*. But that didn't work either. More blocks.

Divine timing was in place though, I just didn't know it at the time.

My Priestess Path Began

I met Julie Parker through Yvette when we had all gathered at a publishing workshop. She greeted me with that same knowing and loving smile that Yvette had done the year before, in all her deliciously pink, floral self. She was the most beautifully feminine woman I'd ever seen. She captivated me, and so I began following her work in the world. This was when I discovered the world of the Priestess. I fell in love with Julie's podcast, *The Priestess Podcast*, instantly. I felt like

I had come home but at such a deeper and rich layer than ever before. Each conversation shared within the podcast literally lit a fire within me so great that I thought my heart would explode and I kept thinking, *how could I possibly find an even deeper exploration into my spiritual journey?*

I found myself expanding in a way that felt so true to me. I knew this was the final, hidden key to untapping all of me. Perhaps even understanding at a greater capacity what my spiritual journey had shown me so far, who I was at a soul-level and what my path forward would be because of it.

Sora Schilling's 'medicine' and work in the world, at that time, was in holding space for and teaching women about sacred circles and ceremonial gatherings. This was, again, such a deeper and richer experience than I could fathom. Her way of interweaving language through the storytelling of soul and her physical presence and way of be-ing when conversing in person with you is something that I can only describe as cosmic—she literally took my breath away the first time I heard her speak. A woman who can stand in her power, unashamedly expressing who she is, what she believes in and does as well as how she wishes for you to expand alongside her too. So, no surprises that when Sora and Julie came together to offer the *Priestess Mistress Mind Temple School* (PMM) the following year, it was a non-negotiable holy-Goddess 'Yes' from me. I knew I had to enrol, just like I knew I had to do Soulpreneurs. Just like I knew I had to move to London. Just like I knew I had to work in food publishing after high school. There are those crossroad choices in life where you have a very clear understanding or knowing of which direction to take and I was at that pivotal point in life. This time I had the full understanding of my intuitive self backing it all up. This wholehearted knowing in heart, mind, body and spirit. It was an easy decision to make. No fear. I was *all* in.

The Priestess path takes you to the depth of who you truly are, even if you feel you're not ready for it. It unlocks so much within that there are times when you don't know which way is up. It's an awakening of self like no other. There are the depths of darkness (the shadow, ego self), and the shining brightness of light (the soul, higher spirit self). There is no end point either, as you soon discover that the path is cyclical, just as we are as be-ings and as our great Goddess, Mother Earth, is too. An ever-changing landscape of self; no end point, a constant spiral of learning, unpacking, doing better and being of our greatest service.

Sora and Julie together in the Temple space of PMM showed me what true Sisterhood could be. Women coming together in all of their facets, showing up authentically as they are with such love and devotion to their teachings. To be held fully by women in a sacred space where you're given full permission to just be you has been the biggest life changing experience for me to date. Without even realising it, I had been longing for this type of Sisterhood my whole life and yet I also intrinsically knew that I had been a part of it before in another lifetime. It was as if my two worlds finally came together—this current life path and my first life path remembering of myself—as a Priestess to the Goddess.

And Now...

To say that I am grateful for the career and thriving business I've had over the past twenty-five years in food publishing is an understatement. I have wholeheartedly loved every year, every experience (even the truly soul-upsetting ones), the gifts received, the financial abundance earned, the global lifestyle I've lived, the flexibility to work in and around birthing our two children and all of this obtained through food, cooking, creating recipes and eating many dishes along the way. It's been a privilege to wake up daily literally busting to get to work and having complete autonomy over how, with whom and what I spent my time on. However, as the years continue to evolve, and I find myself moving slowly between the sacred feminine archetype of Mother to Maga I understand that this shapeshifting of self through the path of the Priestess is a natural one to evolve alongside and deeper into. There's a deeper medicine to come forward now, a connection to the magick mysteries, ancestral land wisdom and devotional spiritual practices to self. And as such, my world of food has shapeshifted alongside it too. I spend my foodie days in business holding space for and guiding women-identifying with their desire for how they nourish themselves with food. Supporting them to stand in food sovereignty. I still create recipes and cookery content, but it's for me and my community spaces only now.

I am in daily, devotional sacred practice with Mother Earth and receive intuitive food-messenger readings from fruits and vegetables that I love to share with my clients and community members. Our kitchen is a temple, a place where we commune as a family and where I gather with others to teach as a collective.

Priestessing in the world for me now looks like what you will read through these pages—a glimpse into the sacred, magickal and delicious world that is food. Food... so much more than what we simply cook and consume. It's sacred, tells ancestral stories, connects us and is the greatest source of loving nourishment to receive from Mother Earth.

I Have a Vision and Mission

My vision is that all of Mother Earth's children—the young and the young that still lives in our hearts—receive the rite of passage that is food sovereignty. To select, cook and eat seasonal food as the spiritual practice it is, so that it becomes an instinctual sacred act that we all do daily to nourish our hearts, minds, bodies and spirits and to reconnect to the infinite source of energy that is Mother Earth. My mission is to support you to reconnect to your intuitive self through understanding your personal cycles, Mother Earth's seasons and the simplicity of delicious food. To finally step away from any food fears and into freedom through saying 'yes' to you in how you choose to select, cook and eat food. This is the greatest act of self-loving care you can give yourself and your community.

Priestess, The Goddess and Seasonal Food

What Is a Priestess?

There are many definitions of a Priestess, from a woman who conducts sacred rites, to a woman who works as a handmaiden to the Goddess or a woman who conducts religious ceremonies.

My personal definition of a Priestess is this:

> *A Priestess is someone who identifies as a woman or holds the flame of the sacred feminine within and has a devotional spiritual practice of their choice, which then allows them to be of greatest service to self, first, so that they can then go out and be of greatest service to others in the world.*

There is no right or wrong way here. The path of the Priestess is as individual to you as your own fingerprints. It's a cyclic journey—no end point, there is constant discovery and deepening into the self—through the shadows and the bright. In the simplest of terms, I view a Priestess as a leader. I believe each and every woman-identifying walking on Mother Earth right now *is* a Priestess. You lead every day, and in every facet, or multi-faceted way, whether you are walking as parent, teacher, healer, space holder, coach, entrepreneur, business owner, lightworker or community member. My intention for you reading this book is that you feel empowered to nourish yourself, as the leader that you are, with food; that you *Priestess Your Plate.*

There are many Goddesses found throughout the world and in most, if not all, traditions. Goddesses were and still are key figures used in sacred celebrations, in devotional sacred practices and for myriad ceremonies. There are Goddesses heavily steeped in food, whether for their individual ties with specific foods just like the Cambodian Rice Goddess, Po Ino Nogar, or in general such as with the Roman Goddess of agriculture, Ceres. Please note that within these pages I have used a different approach to connect the Goddess to food. I've aligned Goddesses to seasonal fruits and vegetables through energetic ways. That is, I've matched the energetic frequency of a Goddess to the same energetic frequency of that fruit or vegetable. This means that you may find a Goddess that is typically known for a certain gift-giving ability, and yet She may show up as another within these pages. Perhaps Her spring energy or gifts also matched a food choice in autumn. Throughout my time over the past four years of working with both Goddesses and food, I've found that this way of connecting them both together provides us with a deeper sense of nourishment, and a greater connection to ourselves as multifaceted be-ings.

This is by no means an overriding of or cultural appropriation of traditional values of the Goddess and how they stand in their original culture as deities, I just wish to express how expansive the Goddess truly is—just as we are—as She is us and we are Her. She resides within us all and is the reflection of all that we are, even if we don't want to see those aspects of self. Think of the food and Goddess initiations as an energetic-frequency match that will unlock the deeper energies within you and how you walk on Mother Earth every day.

The initiations offer great insight into how we can create deeper love, connection, compassion, energy and nourishment through food sacredness.

You as Your Own Sacred Leader, as Priestess

The age of NOW is here.
It's YOUR time.

The sacred ask from Mother Earth is to step fully into your personal power. By reading the pages within this book it already signifies you are on the path Mother Earth asks. One of the greatest ways we can step into our personal power and have an immediate impact on our lives is through food. Food is so much more than just eating to live, eating to gain some sort of result or cooking because we have to, not from a desire to.

Food is true nourishment. Food nourishes the heart, mind, body and spirit. It's our greatest link to our ancestry. It's interwoven through all that we do and achieve while we walk Mother Earth side and it's our greatest, deepest connection we can have with the Great Goddess. When we select, cook and eat seasonal food from Her we are literally enlivening all of our cells with her essence through the fruits, vegetables and other plant products' nutrition that we digest.

Being your own sacred leader is to reclaim sovereignty. Reclaiming food sovereignty is the greatest spiritual act you can do as a divine be-ing. Sovereignty is having the power or authority over self. To become the leader in your home and in your kitchen with food, cooking and eating is to *Priestess Your Plate* through sacred devotion to self. It's food sacredness where the act of selecting, cooking and eating food is viewed as a spiritual practice. When we learn about, understand and then honour where we are at in our sacred feminine cycle of life—maiden, mother, maga, crone—and which cycle of self we are in—blood or moon—we then experience our true self and our personal, authentic energetic needs of heart, mind, body and spirit. To align these personal cycles of self with the seasons of Mother Earth and Her foods is when we thrive and that's what She wants for us—to thrive.

A nourishment like no other, one where we are joyful, feel connected and energised and view ourselves with love and compassion, regardless! Such freedom of self. All through self-empowerment of food.

This is when you become your own sacred leader.

You are a Priestess.

PART *two*
A DELICIOUS BECOMING

Now we explore, unpack and journey a little deeper into YOU.

The Patriarchal Plate

An Important Note

I would like to take this time to preface this section of the book with the following important notes:

There is absolutely nothing wrong with you wanting to improve your health and wellbeing so that you revitalise your heart, mind, body and spirit. If you desire to move easily throughout your day; want to experience sound sleep; and/or be able to feel empowered with how you nourish yourself with food or for any other reason that you desire.

I've personally chosen to honour my body with certain ways of eating and using different types of food so that I can move more easily and 'keep up' with our young children, and also to deepen my connection with Mother Earth. I've specifically found over the past year that my digestive system works much better when I don't eat in the morning or have a big meal late at night. When I feel my energy really falling at turns of the season, I listen and fast for a few hours during the day to reconnect my energy.

The patriarchal plate becomes an area of concern if you're consistently in a state of obsessiveness around food, how you eat, what you eat and when you eat. If your body concerns keep you stuck in the past or you are unable to connect with where you are right now and keep cycling around with the same food-fearing mindset, please honour yourself with seeking further help if this feels true for you.

Food choices that you make should one hundred per cent be coming from a place of alignment with self first, not from what someone else tells you that you *should* be doing (obviously unless from un-biased professional medical teams), or purely for trying to mimic a media-idealised and unattainable body shape. That goes with my words in this book too. These words are true for me; this is your jump-off point to explore *yourself* more.

In my most recent works created in food publishing I have specifically only created recipes for cookbooks with clients I have personally felt are exceptionally heart-centred in their approach with their messaging. This I hold with great integrity, so you may see my name pop up in the back of a few cookbooks over the next couple of years.

Patriarchy

We can't talk about food and the lack of connection we have with it without talking about patriarchy. Patriarchy is *not* an anti-male-identifying movement. It's a system. A system that is upheld just as much by women-identifying, and you can see this heavily in the food, health and wellbeing sector.

Let's look to Wikipedia for a definition of patriarchy:

> *Patriarchy is a social system in which men hold primary power and predominate in roles of political leadership, moral authority, social privilege and*

> *control of property. Some patriarchal societies are also patrilineal, meaning that property and title are inherited by the male lineage.*
>
> *Patriarchy is associated with a set of ideas, a patriarchal ideology that acts to explain and justify this dominance and attributes it to inherent natural differences between men and women. Sociologists tend to see patriarchy as a social product and not as an outcome of innate differences between the sexes and they focus attention on the way that gender roles in a society affect power differentials between men and women.*
>
> *Historically, patriarchy has manifested itself in the social, legal, political, religious and economic organisation of a range of different cultures. Even if not explicitly defined to be by their own constitutions and laws, most contemporary societies are, in practice, patriarchal.*

My belief is that it's the system itself, held by men and women and goes without saying it's steeped in white privilege. So, this isn't about sexes vying against each other, the opposite actually, but it must be mentioned that patriarchal systems have been put in place by the majority, which is white, privileged men, and continues to be upheld by white privilege women. And as you'll read below through the exploration of my personally coined term 'food patriarchy', you will discover that it is gender-neutral and can, and is, upheld by us *all* and affects us *all*.

The Patriarchal Plate

This plate is steeped in fear, holds a linear time frame—you start here, do this and then end here—and is focused on a drastic physical change based on restriction for the sake of vanity, not because of health needs. Messages of health, wellbeing, body shape and size are shared for profit's sake and not for the best outcome for the individual. Your power gets handed over to someone else and you trust everything that they share, with little regard to how you feel or what your innate desires and needs are. Your food sovereignty is handed over. It is malnourishment of the worst kind and strips away your basic human needs for self-empowerment, love and compassion, and your body becomes the enemy. Consistent negative thought patterns on weight, physical shape or ingredient demonising become a vicious cycle that you fear and feel you can't break because you anticipate something 'bad' will happen, such as a change in weight, or a perceived health issue arising. You are led to believe that you don't know what to do and don't have time to do it either.

Writing the paragraph above is hard for me as it is harsh and straight to the point and it brings up a lot of personal experiences for me. I've certainly never been immune to food patriarchy and I believe that you'd have to be a mystical, flying unicorn to have escaped it completely in your lifetime—that's how systemic the problem is.

There are many experiences I've personally had with food and witnessed with so many others, especially those closest to me. But this is the truth; it's what the patriarchal plate is. It's why we've become so disconnected to one of life's basic needs—food. FOOD. Food grown by our Great Goddess,

Mother Earth. It's why I have witnessed women in my family literally starving themselves, constantly comparing their body to others and consistently outwardly shaming themselves for the food they eat, when they eat it and what they would do to correct what they had eaten. It's why as a teenager I wouldn't let anyone see me eat and why I layered on clothes to hide my body shape. It's why I couldn't quite understand that after having birthed two very healthy children at the age of thirty-eight that my body shape just couldn't "bounce back" to what it was when I was twenty-nine years old, or like every magazine/celebrity/women's article said it could or should if I only did x, y, z (with a newborn and toddler in tow!). It's why the health and wellbeing sector is a multi-trillion-dollar industry. Let's read that sentence again. A MULTI-TRILLION-dollar industry. It's why we are carrying more weight—emotionally, physically, mentally and spiritually—and yet are starved of actual nourishment, feel disconnected and lack energy.

We've been fed lies from big corporations in the food industry for decades that has government backing purely for financial reasons and mass-market share. We are specifically marketed to our 'pain points' to purchase products we don't need or want. There are people creating content for you to digest who don't actually cook or are even interested in cooking; having your name published on a cookbook has become the new business card in the industry.

We're fed the illusion that we are time-poor so we can't possibly cook a homemade meal and turn to convenience foods, yet spend hours scrolling through social media every night. We consume more food reality TV and cooking shows today and yet we order more take-out meals than ever before. It's why the number-one question I get asked when people find out what my business is, is, 'So what do you eat?' and then the annoyance I see in their faces when I reply with, 'Well, it depends on the season and how I'm feeling on the day…' I know they are really wanting to hear me say, 'Well, I'm carb-free, sugar-free, grain-free…' or whatever the trend is at the time.

I share all of this not to cast shame or call out anyone in particular, it's just where we are at and to highlight that you have the ultimate power. You are a deliciously intuitive being. Everyone has just lost their way because of how much 'noise' is out there in the world. We've all been in these spaces at some point in our lives. I have too. I am certainly someone who hasn't been immune to it. I've also been someone who has worked in the food publishing industry and seen it all rise from where it initially was when I first started decades ago. I still find it completely absurd that we were fed the idea that a blueberry is a more idealised fruit than an apple—an apple! The original fruit of the Goddess! The amount of shame I have heard in the voices from parents when they have told me that they can't afford to feed their children blueberries all the time was my end point with it *all*.

How on Mother Earth did we get to this point? This point where two fruits are depicted against each other, and online social media 'wars' are started in the comments of posts around this. This is the patriarchal plate and what it does. It sells an ideal that's unattainable and then shames you into believing you're doing something wrong because you don't follow the perceived rule, or you get socially outed. It keeps the energetic cords of the sister wound well and truly alive and thriving, and if you're unsure of what I mean here then all you need do is take a look on any woman-identifying health, wellbeing or food forum and simply read the comments, judgements and personal attacks made on community members around food choices, especially when it has to do with losing weight or feeding children.

No wonder we're at this point. We've become oversaturated and overstimulated by the world of food media with body image in general too. This crisis point we are now in has us so confused about what to do, how to do it, what's good, what's bad, lending us to thoughts like, *What do I feed the children? I don't know how to cook. Why isn't my body the same weight after the children? What's wrong with me?...* on and on and on.

As someone who has worked in the food publishing industry for twenty-five consecutive years, I have definitely seen myriad food and dietary trends come and go. I was there at the start of the rise of the celebrity chef, which was then followed by the rise of the celebrity 'home cook' through reality TV and cooking shows, that then led to the rise of celebrity social media influencers, many of which have no food, dietary, nutritional or other related professional qualifications, despite that others do. I have written best-selling cookbooks for most of them here in Australia.

I've seen every which way possible an influencer try to convince me that their way isn't a damaging diet but instead a lifestyle choice, yet it still comes with a set of terms and conditions, dos and don'ts for you to follow, that strip away your sovereignty in actually choosing food that's aligned with you. Again, there are others out there, albeit few of them, that will help guide you to understanding what to do for you. But there are no sales in publishing if you actually teach people how to nourish themselves, they simply wouldn't need to buy another product again, would they? It's all the same, whichever package it comes wrapped up in a bow with. It's making money by instilling food fear that has generational impacts that will take decades to correct. Decades! People being steered so far away from their true sense of who they are, how their body feels and how to nourish themselves with food. The art of cooking being completely lost.

People generally don't know how to menu plan, budget for food or store items correctly, which then just ends up as masses of food waste, or only have basic cookery skills in the kitchen, not knowing what flavours work best with each other. Generational and ancestral storytelling through food is almost extinct in the majority of western families. The most upsetting part that I have witnessed over time is that through all of this over-saturation of food patriarchy, the greatest disservice it has done to us all is that it's taken us further away from, and out of, our kitchens. It's become a food space in the home that's labelled as too hard or too time-consuming, a daily task without enjoyment, something that has to be done and not out of want or desire. Just look at the aesthetic change to kitchens over the years and you'll see what I mean. The heart and soul of the home being transformed from a delicious family all-in working space to sleek and minimalist, where you can't even tell there's a kitchen there! Now, don't get me wrong, I love living as minimal a life as possible, but I also want to be able to easily see and find a fridge, stovetop and kitchen sink too. And this is what children are seeing, feeling and are surrounded by.

Basic skills are being or have been completely lost and there are no consistent practical cookery classes in schools to close the gap either. The art of ancestral cooking and the handing down of cultural recipes and heirloom cookery items is almost non-existent. Food has become fast, cheap, available 24/7 and so overly commercialised that some of it isn't actually safe for human consumption… and don't get me started on those 'frankenfoods' (that's for another book perhaps!). Again, I don't write these words to alarm or instil even more fear. But these conversations need to be had. We cannot create change if we cannot see where the problem lies. We cannot reclaim our power if we cannot see where we've knowingly, or unknowingly, handed it away. And we cannot expand into the fullness of who we truly are and what we are here to do if we don't know how to nourish our whole selves with food.

The great news is today is a new day and from this point on, small daily acts can create immense change over time.

My Aha Moment
This was one of the greatest catalysts for me stepping away from writing for the health and wellbeing market. I actually saw and felt in myself the changes over the past ten years of being so immersed in these cookbooks I was writing, literally living and breathing all these mixed messages month after

month from the content I was creating, to the testing of those recipes to eat and onto the cooking of them at photo shoots.

Not one of my clients or publishers have ever known this about me, but every single recipe I've ever written, every cookbook I've created from scratch and every piece of food information I've produced for others over these years, has only ever come from my intuition as an embodied experience. I dive headfirst into embracing the experience of whatever it is that I'm writing about—gluten-free, paleo, keto, high protein, low carb, diabetic—you name it, I've written and lived it. What happened to me over those ten years is that I became disconnected and angry; I wasn't aligned, I gained eighteen kilos, I had no clue who I was anymore. I realised I had become the end product of all of those mixed food publishing messages. I couldn't believe I had done that to myself—me of all people. And that scared the living shyte outta me!

If I so easily and deceivingly fell into that trap, even with all of my knowledge, then no wonder people out there were so conflicted—feeling worse and worse and completely at wit's end, until the next new food trend popped up. Always searching for that next big foodie fix. And whoa, did that hit me hard. I knew that if I felt this way, no wonder people were so lost, no wonder nobody enjoyed cooking anymore, no wonder people just have no idea what to eat anymore, no wonder people started to see a berry as more important than an apple and no wonder we hold so much fear, are disconnected, lethargic and just stuck. To be honest, no-one has the energy to get out of it.

Food Privilege

The most vicious part of all of this food patriarchy is the food privilege I've witnessed over the years, and still do in some online spaces. And just when I think I've removed myself from them all, another post or comment pops up and shows me how systemic it all is. It goes without saying here that this privilege comes from the same people who live with white privilege daily. Food privilege is the demonising of foods, ways of eating and even how you cook against each other.

Overtly highlighting that only organic, biodynamic and non-supermarket bought groceries are better than others. Don't get me wrong here, I am completely aware of the damage to our bodies and our environment from pesticide-heavy foods, the impact on local farmers because of big food corps and the myriad other effects attached to this. But standing on a moral high ground and demonising others for not converting or doing the same is the issue. Be an activist by all means, but don't stand in your privilege and blame or shame others because they're not following suit.

When we had our firstborn, we were down to one minimal wage and paying a mortgage. There were some weeks where we lived off white rice and cans of lentils because money was so tight. This was my wake-up call to the food privilege I had been walking with up until that point. It was an eye-opener for sure. It's a privilege to be able to afford to purchase basic food needs, fresh ingredients to cook with and to have every family member be able to eat full meals together. Not the parents or carers going hungry so that the children can at least eat. It absolutely breaks my heart and makes me feel sick that this still happens, especially when we live in a world where the food, health and wellbeing sector is a multi-trillion-dollar industry. We literally have people who can't afford to eat living among those who deem an $8 biodynamic punnet of berries as social status.

The 'Avocado Effect'

With being able to witness the rise and fall of so many food trends over the years, along with witnessing women close to me battle with food, cooking and eating, there is another key thing to add to this part of our conversation—and that's science. With technology constantly on the rise and science seemingly going in leaps and bounds each year, food has been one of those items where we've seen immense expansion. I vividly remember in the eighties as a child hearing the women of our neighbourhood talk about how bad avocado was for you. The amount of fat was outrageous to them so it was a non-existent fruit on our barbecue tables. I remember thinking, *But it grows on a tree, how can that be bad?*

Fast forward a couple of decades and you can't go anywhere without avocado being on the menu or gracing the pages of magazines and cookbooks. Through the evolution of science, how we look at food has changed so much over the years with avocado now hailed for its health benefits and labelled a superfood. This is another term I've never understood either because #ItsGrownOnATree and aren't all plant foods grown by Mother Earth super anyway! So I've termed this the 'avocado effect'. It's true that we only know what we know at the time given the capabilities to understand as humans, but I do think quite often about what we will laugh about in another couple of decades when it comes to food... perhaps like, *Oh do you remember when people turned against potatoes, breads and pastas for so many years?*

OK, Tracey, What Is the Difference Here with *Priestess Your Plate*?

The Priestess Plate is literally the opposite to all of the above! YEP. It honours YOU. It empowers you to be your own teacher or healer or guru, to trust your own intuition and to understand yourself, your needs and how to nourish yourself with food; how to nurture yourself with food through honouring your personal cycles of self within the seasons of Mother Earth. Reconnecting to your ancestry and where you reside.

It is nonlinear and time doesn't exist because there is no start or end... it's ever evolving, expanding or contracting, right alongside of you, because we are all cyclic be-ings. It can change in an instant or not at all. It's based on love and compassion for self, first and foremost, and then for others and our Great Mother Earth. Its honouring our whole selves and the current sacred feminine cycle we are moving through—maiden, mother, maga or crone—with the pure understanding that we shift and change throughout our lives, especially as we age.

When you *Priestess Your Plate* your body is honoured for who She is given where you're at in your life. We don't stay stuck in the past. We honour where we're at today and hold the gratitude and privilege of what it means to be able to look forward into the future. The easiest example of what I mean here is to explain it through a story about jeans. Yes, jeans—those size 8, super skinny, tight, overly priced, designer jeans that I wore in my late twenties. As gorgeous as they were (and I certainly got my money's worth out of them), it's inconceivable for me to consider holding onto them in the hope that I may wear them again more than two decades later and especially after birthing two very healthy children, each weighing almost 5 kilograms as newborns, and the change in my hip structure since.

To *Priestess Your Plate* is a birthright. There is a rite of passage with food. It's about understanding the process and knowing that every choice you make when it comes to food comes from your heart and brings you back home to yourself. The difference for me, with my sacred knowledge and experience, my food medicine, my beliefs, my vision and mission, is that I actually want change to occur.

I want to see you empowered; I want you to feel nourished with what I create here. I want you to understand that you have it all within you already. We will reignite your intuition again. To open you up further to the pure magick that food is. How it connects us to ourselves, to others, to community and to our great Goddess, Mother Earth.

As people read this book, I want them to rediscover themselves, journey deep into their food stories, reconnect to their whole selves and finally reclaim food sovereignty so that once they've laid their own food foundation and taken dedicated action steps forward, they'll never hand over their power again to any other food fad or trend. I want them to get excited about cooking again! We are turning the clock back to how delicious it used to be—to the simplicity of food, seasonal cooking and eating intuitively. Do no harm to self, or to others culturally or to the land where you reside.

Cycles of Self and Seasons of Mother Earth

Cycles of Self

It's important to note that as we journey through each cycle, our cycle can shift and change within the hour, days, weeks or years, through our blood cycles or by the lunar cycles, and of course through Mother Earth's seasons too.

Your Energy 'Bodies'

Oh, I talk a lot about these as we are made up of all four of these components and to just focus solely on one of them at a time doesn't do us any justice or nourish us. Your energy bodies, or energetic bodies, are those subtle layers of self—the components that make up the whole of you. Now, in eastern philosophy there are more than four discussed and without doing harm, or culturally appropriating that system (as it's not from my ancestry), I choose to work with the four that are most present in our daily lives and that which we can easily work with and tap into at any point throughout the day.

> *Please note: I interchange the terms emotional body, mental body, physical body and spiritual body with heart, mind, body and spirit through the pages of this book.*

Sacred Feminine Cycles

I've learned quite a lot from Jane Hardwicke Collings and the sacred work she does with women throughout each of their life stages.

There are four sacred feminine cycles of life that women journey through while walking on Mother Earth and they are the following, as described by Jane:

Rite of Passage	Life Season	Rite of Passage	Age	Mother Earth's Season
birth	Maiden	menarche	0-25	spring
childbirth	Mother	menopause	25-50	summer
menopause	Maga	retirement	50-70	autumn
retirement	Crone	death	70-100+	winter

Mother Earth's Seasons

Spring, summer, autumn and winter each come to us with a completely different energy expression and to honour them as they come and go is to honour ourselves deeply.

> *In spring, we come alive and feel*
> *invigorated by the emerging light.*
> *In summer, we celebrate ourselves out in the*
> *world in the fullness of ourselves in the sun.*
> *In autumn, we replenish through letting*
> *go and restore in preparation.*
> *In winter, we go within and deeply surrender*
> *into, and trust, the darkness.*

A fast-paced modern-day life can have your four energetic bodies (heart, mind, body and spirit) running in summer busy mode for the entirety of a full year. Before you realise, exhaustion kicks in, your immunity becomes weak, your adrenals are heightened and any opportunity your body gets when you finally slow down and rest (usually when on your first holiday break for the year), you get sick with whatever bug is floating around. If this sounds like you, don't worry—I've been there right with you. I personally did this year in, year out, for a very long time!

As you'll discover throughout *Priestess Your Plate*, the available energy to us in each season is, again, another way Mother Earth is showing us best how we can support ourselves through Her nurturing. She is literally making the conditions for which we live in throughout each season, have you reprogram yourself to be in cyclic alignment with Her.

> *As another old-time saying goes:*
> *Mother knows best!*

In spring the sun awakens again; our creative self rises as we start to bloom into our full selves, and we desire to smell and taste the new season's produce.

Summer expresses the intensity of the sun, and for long periods of time, and we naturally want to commune outside bathing in all its glory while cooling down from the inside out through raw foods and sweet fruits.

In autumn we begin to mature and start to let go as we head indoors from the cooler days; we bear witness to the tree change and warm from within using slightly cooked fruits and simmered vegetables.

Winter expresses the intensity of the darkness and we naturally want to hide away, cocooning ourselves indoors for longer periods of time with our loved ones while devouring slow-cooked root vegetables to keep us grounded and rich desserts that touch our soul.

Solstice and Equinox

I couldn't possibly write this sacred book without highlighting that as I deepen my Priestess work with Mother Earth, I also find myself wanting to deepen my celebrations of Her seasons too—year in, year out.

These following four solar cycles we honour are held on the following days in the Southern Hemisphere and Northern Hemisphere:

Spring Equinox (or Ostara): 21–22 September / 21–22 March
Summer Solstice (or Litha): 21–22 December / 21–22 June
Autumn Equinox (or Mabon): 21–22 March / 21–22 March
Winter Solstice (or Yule): 21–22 June / 21–22 December

There are a further four religious, seasonal cycles:
Imbolc (2 Aug / 2 Feb)
Beltane (1 Nov / 1 May)
Lughnasadh (1 Feb / 1 Aug)
Samhain (30 Apr / 31 Oct)

All of which, when added to the four solar cycles, complete 'The Wheel of The Year.' This is the symbol of the eight festivals and celebrations honoured by the ancient practices of Paganism and Wicca.

Now there simply aren't enough pages of this book to offer further explorations into each of these celebrations at each turn of the wheel, but do know that I honour them through my own food sacredness and spiritual practices and speak openly about these in my community spaces.

Where I Am At
Every day, week, month, season, year, decade and so on I am an ever-changing, multifaceted spiritual soul, be-ing human. It's taken the majority of my life to figure this one out. That I can hold the energy of each season in an hour, a day, a week, a year, a decade either all at once, as a singular or none at all. As such, I prefer to wake each day with the understanding that I will hold the energy that needs to be held in each moment. There are those winter times when I retreat heavily and want to be away from the world. The times of full summer where I want to be out socialising in groups. The between times like autumn's Maga energy where I simply want to reflect, create or let go. All in one or none at all.

Personally, I am deep in the cycle of the 'Mother' with our two young, primary school-aged children and yet I am already experiencing and hearing the call of the Maga pull me forward as I've been moving through perimenopause over the past eighteen months and all of me is heightened at this cycle—intuition, sensitivities and emotions.

As a practising Priestess I feel I transverse between all four archetypes of Maiden, Mother, Maga and Crone. Depending on the season we are journeying through on Mother Earth at the time, in each season She offers me another level to explore—whether that be through inner child work during the Maiden energy of spring or exploring my untapped crone witchyness during winter. Cancerian born and on the day that is Goddess Cerridwen's celebration day, July 3, I am ruled by the moon—the element of water, magick and the sacred cauldron. So as you can imagine my emotions can flow freely and again, depending on what season we are cycling through with Mother Earth, this flow state can either be in contraction or expansion and I take great comfort in, and have an immense passion for, my sacred cauldron work that is the craft of creating and cooking food. And as two of my closest spirit Sisters and I constantly share together… #YouJustCantMakeThisShitUp

I also recognise deeply the fact that I walk on Mother Earth daily as a privileged white woman and as such I have a daily spiritual practice that is dedicated to anti-racism education. I pay for educational services created by First Nations, Black, Indigenous and People of Colour. I listen deeply, donate and, most importantly, I take action.

As you begin to discover your own personal cycles and how these interweave with Mother Earth's seasons, you too will begin to see how simple it is to use food sacredness as a daily spiritual practice. How you can honour yourself as a sacred leader, as the Priestess of your own plate.

Food Sacredness: Selecting, Cooking and Eating as Spiritual Practice

I talk a lot about food sacredness, and it can cover many facets of our journey with food, but in its simplest explanation it's food as spiritual practice that is sacred to you and meets you where you're at.

A devotional service to self that moves beyond that buzz term 'self-care', as it becomes community-care, a much deeper impact because of the conscious loving and compassionate way *you* nourish *you*. When we walk daily as nourished, loving and compassionate be-ings we radiate this energy out into the world and what we radiate out has an incredible impact on others. Everything is energy! Your heart space frequency, your vibration, can be scientifically 'read' and is referred to as Energetic Communication (or cardio electromagnetic communication).

And this doesn't have to be an orchestrated affair either or again a formula of selecting, eating and cooking a certain way, religiously. It's honouring your heart and what you desire above all else. All it takes is understanding, trust, surrender, grace and giving it all a seasoning of delicious love. It's taking the everyday act of selecting, cooking and eating food and turning it into a sacred, spiritual practice, whether you cook for yourself each day, within a family unit or with others in a shared house.

Now, you may be thinking, *Hang on there, Trace, are you losing your mind? I've got young children at home, I can't even consider what to cook for dinner most nights, let alone turning it into some spiritual practice... this sounds unachievable to me.*

Oh, I hear you, delicious one, and that's a little bit of food patriarchy creeping in there that will have you believe it's unachievable; that you don't have the skills, knowledge, time or interest. It is OK—food patriarchy has programmed us all into believing such things. But it's simply not true. You can do this, and very easily too. I've got you covered because I'm in the same boat. I'm a mum running my own business (there ain't no team behind me, yet!), I have a hubby that works six long days a week in a high-pressure job and two small children who have a way more exciting social and sports calendar than I do. A true COO of the household. And yet, I believe and actively do advocate that there is a path to self-actualisation through food, and that it's really simple for us all to achieve.

It starts with viewing food and understanding that it is sacred, seeing how we can select, cook and eat as a spiritual practice first and foremost.

First, let's read another golden nugget from good-old wikipedia.com about the meaning of spiritual practice:

> *A spiritual practice or spiritual discipline is the regular or full-time performance of actions and activities undertaken for the purpose of inducing spiritual experiences and cultivating spiritual development.*

Let's break this down. Food is a basic need that we are in action with every single day. At every meal opportunity we can elevate our whole selves (in heart, mind, body and spirit) through that food. So my question to you then is, how can you not have food be a daily spiritual practice? Again, this isn't a call to completely flip what you eat on its head, start to restrict food items or overburden yourself with a whole new cupboard's worth of praised foods or cooking items. It's small, positive steps forward in your mindset through aligned action to create an authentic experience for self that has an empowering outcome. Now I just know you want a piece of that! (Pardon the pun…) So, have a read below for a little toolkit of ways in which I, and we as a family, create food sacredness daily through the spiritual practice of selecting, cooking and eating food.

Selecting Food as Spiritual Practice

Giving Thanks
Look at the food you select and give thanks to all the people who made it possible for you to be selecting it, from the farmers to growers, packers, transport people, cashiers etc.

Intuition
You may already do this and just not be aware of it! When you select certain fruits or vegetables your hand naturally always gravitates to the energetically matched pieces that you end up buying. If you have children, have them do this for you, without questioning their choices, as children are more intuitive than most of us adults are.

Mindfulness
Understanding where the product you purchase is coming from, given where you reside, and the impact it has on Mother Earth.

Simplicity
Remembering that a few simple ingredients can make a great meal.

Affirmations
I am nourished by the food I receive.

Angels
Call in Archangels, Ascended Masters or your own angelic council to be with you.

Community
Get out and about in your community, go to open-air markets and talk to the farmers and growers themselves.

Walking Meditation
Pop in earphones and listen to guided meditations while you shop and select.

Garden
Give your hand at growing your own food; starting with herbs is a great place.

Crystals
Place crystals into your pockets, purse or in your bra that can either ground your energy or enliven you, if needed.

Sovereignty
Feel empowered in how, where and when you choose to use your money when purchasing.

Cooking Food as Spiritual Practice

Speak
Say out loud your gratitude for having heat to cook with, running clean water to use and an able body that can move easily around a kitchen to cook. Adding voice to these amplifies the energy behind them and it's an incredible gift for your children or loved ones to hear you cultivate gratitude.

Chant
Sing or chant powerful phrases or words; look to each season's offers to start you off or create your own.

Ritual
Have a ritual around how you cook in the kitchen. Set your chopping board, gather your tools, then the ingredients. Work in a way that becomes second nature, without rushing.

Service
To cook food is to be of service to self and others and is an absolute gift.

Ceremonial Space
Set your kitchen space up as if you're stepping into a sacred ceremony. Have candles lit, some picked flowers or herbs visible, soft music playing and even spritz yourself with a calming essential oils blend.

Ancestors
Call in your ancestors to your kitchen space or simply chat to them about your day, either in your mind's eye or out loud.

Dance
Turn the music on or pop those earphones in and dance away while you prepare and cook. Your body will tingle all over and the food will join in on the fun.

Heart Connection
When you cook, you are using your hands, and your hands are directly linked to and connect with your heart chakra space.

Herbs
Fresh or dried herbs are so magickal to use in your cooking as they hold a high vibration of energy. Plus, they're the simplest way of injecting huge amounts of flavour into meals, will make any dish look vibrant and delicious and have you claim the kitchen witch that you are.

Flowers
Flowers add energy, fragrance and a delight to your eyes and will lift your kitchen space instantly and make you smile.

Heirloom
Use any sacred heirloom tools or cookery items such as pans or bowls to invoke the energy of ancestral food storytelling.

Eating as Spiritual Practice

Offerings
Cultivate blessings, prayers of invocations to food ingredients before eating or when sharing meals with others.

Space
Put great thought to where furniture items are placed for enjoying meals and that spaces are uncluttered so that when you sit or stand to eat there is better flow.

Letting Go
Simply letting go of all your preconceived notions on what or how to eat is a spiritual practice of release that is powerful.

Memories
Reflect back on and discuss openly food memories from childhood.

Storytelling
Share ancestral food stories and cultural dishes from the past, especially if you have children who didn't experience these through great-grandparents or grandparents.

Creativity
Now you don't need to be a professional food stylist here but thinking about how you place food items onto plates or into bowls can have an incredible effect on your senses. It's a feast for your eyes!

Discernment
This is incredibly empowering to you and for your children when you sit down to share meals together. Place all the food at the centre of a table and allow each person to discern what and how much they would like to eat. I've personally found that our children try more things, eat more vegetables than usual and you can see how empowered they are when they finally master using serving tools like sets of tongs.

Dark Night of The Soul
Yes, this will and does occur to us all. When it comes to eating at these times your greatest spiritual practice is to simply allow, trusting that this cycle will end at some point and that when you surrender to your body's needs at this time you're nourishing it so much more than if you were to restrict it.

Laughter
Make eating at mealtimes light and a safe place for you to commune with others through fun topics of conversation where laughter is predominant.

Grounding
Consciously plant your feet securely on the ground, whether you stand or sit down to eat, and think of a golden cord coming out from your feet that travels down into the soil of Mother Earth. Asking to be held as you start to enjoy your meal is such a simple way to ground your energy, especially if it's been a more than stressful day.

Inner Thought
Simply thinking great words of appreciation for the food that you are about to enjoy offers a deeper level of nourishment. *Oh, look how cute those baby carrots are. Wow, don't they taste so sweet too!*

You can clearly see here that there are myriad ways you can easily create food sacredness in your daily life through spiritual practice. I'd love for you to explore and share with me your findings when you do (as I know you will)—your own personal way of doing this. Look to your ancestral lines and culture around food, think back to memories of what you saw when loved ones or friends cooked when you were growing up. There is a delicious world for you to explore and to create your own kitchen toolkit with.

One thing you may have noticed is that I *haven't* shared above a prescription of what exact types of food to eat and when. This is your choice. All I can offer you is this: When you select, cook and eat foods that are available in the season you are currently cycling through, using one, some or many (or whatever else you discover along the way) from the kitchen toolkit above, your mindset will shift to a loving, compassionate relationship alongside food. It will hold deeper meaning for you and food sacredness will become something you look forward every day.

Heart-Mapping Your Journey

This is the section where I'm most excited for you to journey into—a heart-mapping of you. Here you will be able to gently unpack further your own delicious journey of food. Please be aware that as you journey further into your story, you could experience some activations that are unsettling. Please seek further guidance from a trained professional counsellor or therapist if you find that your thoughts around any of these topics keep you feeling deeply stuck in the past and unable to move forward.

This is a space and time for reflection to see briefly where thoughts, ideas or beliefs have come from and if they still feel true to who you are now, today, and then where you can go to from this point forward.

Be sure to work through these prompts from your heart space, not the ego mind. Your heart will always come through with loving guidance, not fear, and most often is that quieter voice from within you, not that loud, overriding voice we tend to hear first.

Before you get started though, I welcome you to head to www.traceypattison.com/pyp-book to download the *Sacred Food Journey Meditation* before you take these prompts for reflecting on and journaling with. It will be a way for you to ground your energy deeply to Mother Earth and be sure that all four of your energetic bodies are sitting in a space of clarity before you begin.

Enjoy this sacred time of you!

> **Start Here and See Where It Takes You**
>
> Where do your own beliefs, traditions and stories come from with food? Think of family, friends and relationships you've had in the past or are still in.
>
> What can you let go of? In terms of how you select food, cook and eat.
>
> How can you unpack your own food privilege? Where are your biases?
>
> What is actually true for you in terms of food?
>
> How do you like to shop, cook and eat?
>
> Where are you today, and where can you expand from?

Reflect on stories you think to yourself or say out loud constantly, such as:

> *I don't have time.*
> *I don't know how.*
> *I just don't like it.*
> *My children won't eat what I make anyway.*

Keep an open heart with this; this is deep work that will touch your heart, mind, body and spirit. Always hold the understanding that we all have food shadows, we all have stories whether gathered by our own free will or whether we've adopted them from those around us or closest to us.

Your BFF when working through these questions is your journal. Write freely and without judgement for self—this is where you get to fully express all of who you are and you don't have to read it back if you wish not to. This is your personal, sacred time to explore all of you, without any filter.

You can find further resources and a full (and delicious looking) *Heart-Mapping Your Journey Guide* at www.traceypattison.com/pyp-book if you choose to journey deeper.

PART *three*
SEASONAL FOOD AND GODDESS INITIATIONS

Seasonal Food

Seasonal food gives us the opportunity to connect with many aspects of the Goddess through the cycles of seasons and, depending on the food we choose and the way we cook, we can create myriad energetic imprints to truly nourish our hearts, minds, bodies and spirits. Remembering that all of this energy (the season, the food and the Goddess) is held daily by the greatest Goddess of all, Mother Earth—She is our tangible, devoted Mother who is always there holding us in a deep embrace of love.

Just think of your cells receiving Her energetic imprint through the food that She grows for us. There truly is no deeper connection, no greater grounding practice to receive from Her than that.

Discover the true magick of food and the sacred 'medicine' messages that the seasonal plant foods shared in this section of the book wish to communicate with you. The seasonal fruits and vegetables that wanted to be chosen in these pages, along with their energetic Goddess matchings, will give you a deeper understanding of who they are and how they can be of greater service to you daily, within the season you are currently cycling through. This will be information that may come to you by complete surprise or you may find an instant connection.

Please note I have based these foods on where I reside, which is the land if the Gadigal People of the Eora nation (considered the Inner West of coastal Sydney), in Australia. Some of these foods may be true for you also where you reside in the same season, or they may not. Get to know what is best grown local and seasonally in the area you reside.

It is also important to note here that your own acknowledgment of who the traditional owners and custodians of the land, the sky and waterways of where you live be known. I firmly believe that you will never feel completely grounded on the land where you work, live and commune on until this information is known to you. Do the work to find this out for yourself and your loved ones if it's not already known. This is not about culturally appropriating another's culture, its recognition that sovereignty has never been ceded.

I've used the four most widely recognised western seasons here too, and where you reside on Mother Earth will influence how each of these either expand or contract more for you. Simply find a place within this section that suits your environment best.

In each season you will see that I have broken them down further into the three tangible months of:

First month Rising
>In the first month of the season, we slowly rise into Her energy, as we acknowledge that we are still in a release phase of the previous season just journeyed through.

Second month Surrender
> In the second month we've crossed the threshold and are fully into the energy of the season, as this is a time marked by the passing of either the celebrations of equinox or solstice. Equinox marks equal hours of both sunlight and dark. Solstice marks when the sun is highest (summer) or at its lowest (winter) point in the sky.

Third month Emerging
> In the third month we begin our emergence out of the season and start to ready ourselves. This point in every season is where we can start to feel energetically like we are in transition, holding one foot deeply in the past and eager to step the other foot into the future.

It is here where we create and connect—with our hands and heart. My most favourite part of all, around food sacredness as a spiritual practice, is to cook with my hands while holding the intention of the energy I desire for myself and for those that will eat the food created. It's a totally delicious experience from start to end.

When we create with our hands, we are connecting with our heart chakra space and this automatically infuses love into all that we do. Now think of how delicious that is when you've selected produce by hand, prepared food by hand, cooked with your hands and then eat it too.

I like to think that the common phrases 'made with love' or 'cooked with love' have come from this knowledge of the immense energetic imprint we can have, especially when shared with others, connecting us directly through our hearts. I was incredibly fortunate to grow up in a household where I enjoyed food from both sets of my grandparents' kitchens. There was always so much love infused into the food we ate and that food offered joy to everyone involved in the preparing and cooking process.

In each of the classic four seasons explored in *Priestess Your Plate*, you will see at the start of each seasonal initiation section there are notes, ideas, invitations and explorations specific to that season. These are further offerings for you to explore in addition to how you select, cook and eat as spiritual practice.

A great wish I hold for you is that selecting, cooking and eating seasonal food while connected to your whole self (in heart, mind, body and spirit) becomes a daily spiritual practice for you. That you ignite your intuition on how you desire to be nourished so that you can feel empowered, energised and connected through the love and compassion you have shown your whole self through eating as you desire. Basically, I'd love for you to feel and experience food as I do daily—with passion, fun, love and so much joy for the utter gift it truly is and then be able to witness that in others when you cook food for them too. #HeartExplosion

When I select, cook and eat food it's always done with simplicity and always honours the fresh produce where it's at—no complicated methods or overly extensive ingredients lists. You will find this reflected in my recipes shared in this section of the book. I look forward to your feedback when you take the action with your hands to cook these, so please share with me words of your experience with them and any photos you take! Refer back to page 9 where I share how you can connect further with me as you journey through this sacred text.

Seasonal Goddesses
Given that my ancestry is steeped in Celtic and Slavic traditions you will notice that at the start of each seasonal initiation I have shared an overarching Goddess that feels true to me and my lineage and one that sat alongside me as I wrote the words to that seasonal section. Please take time to explore the world of the Goddess through your own ancestry too, to see if you can connect to Her at a deeper level, along with the food.

The Initiations
This is your initiation into the world of seasonal food and the Goddess and one that I know exceptionally well and work alongside daily, so I welcome you into this very sacred space. This is the beginning point for you to discover the true magick that is available to you daily through simple, humble, seasonal food.

Please note that in each of the Seasonal Food and Goddess Initiations, the Goddesses that wanted to be aligned with the fruits and vegetables have come forward as they're an energetic match. Each of these Goddesses are honoured and celebrated through their cultural traditions for myriad reasons, but here we are taking a modern approach guided purely by the plant food messengers themselves.

Enjoy this exploration; play with it, see what lands personally for you, what you invoke and what doesn't land. As mentioned many times throughout the book, be empowered by your *own* path to food sacredness to truly discover what resonates deeply. A great indication here of what suits you best will be the fact that you will find something really easy to understand and simple to do without much thought or push behind doing so. You'll feel an instant connection. Those things that are not energetically aligned will simply fall away, remembering once again that when you *Priestess Your Plate* there are no right or wrong ways of doing things.

Give yourself *full* permission to explore and surrender into each delicious experience, your life will be so much richer for it.

Now, let's dive deeply into the seasons of Mother Earth and the energetic and magickal world of Food and Goddess Initiations. I so wish that I could physically be with you in person to witness these explorations but know that I am cheerleading you on while holding you in my heart.

SPRING

Spring Food and Goddess Initiations

Spring Is...
Fresh beginnings; planting the seeds; childlike joy; sprouting ideas, thoughts and actions; blooming into our whole selves; cleansing and activating the new; rising into 'freshness'; smelling the sweetness of life; awakening to the return of the sun.

Sacred feminine energy for spring is the Maiden: the embodiment of passion and youthful play, speaker of truths, blossoming into beauty, intuitive childhood fantasies.

> **Spring magick**
> **Moon cycle is** first quarter
> **Element is** air
> **Direction is** east
> **Time of day is** dawn
> **Tools are** personal intuition and using the wand
> **Colours are** whites and all pastel colours

Kitchen Craft for Spring
Start to view your kitchen, the heart and soul of your home, as one big altar. The one sacred, temple space where you and your loved ones can commune together. Try these kitchen (altar) crafts throughout spring:

Make a fresh herb and edible flower mandala on your kitchen bench or dining table. Allow it to hold the space for you and loved ones to commune around while preparing food or eating at mealtimes.

Using kitchen twine, weave together bundles of herbs and edible flowers while speaking prayer to form a seasoning stick that you can hang above your stove when cooking. The steam will engulf the bundle and perfume the air, therefore spreading throughout your home the intentional prayer.

Empowering Words
You can speak these words out loud, write them down in your journal or post them up on your fridge for added personal empowerment through springtime. Try these to begin, and then have a go at writing your own too.

> *I allow my beautiful self to bloom.*
> *I receive the new, joyfully.*
> *I create with passion.*

Spring Seasoning: Awakening Salt
This is the dedicated seasoning blend for spring and can be used to season vegetables and proteins of choice before or after cooking.

Make this salt fresh each time as needed, and discard any remains not used by throwing them over your left shoulder into the garden while giving thanks. Combine together 2 tablespoons of pink sea salt flakes + finely grated rind of 1 small orange + 1 teaspoon celery seeds + 1 tablespoon freshly picked thyme leaves.

Serves 2–4.

Overarching Goddess Dedication: Celtic Goddess Brigid
Goddess Brigid worked with me very gently and unwaveringly when I sat down to write this delicious section of the book. Her sacred flame lit that inner fire or spark within me to create further. I found a focused, inner strength that I've never experienced before. There was a sense of poetic flow and the words easily transcribed from thought to keyboard for you. I found myself wanting to enjoy eating more artisan-style breads and ferociously devoured freshly podded peas and avocado sandwiches piled high with sprouts of all sorts.

> More Spring Goddesses
> **Welsh Goddess Blodeuwedd** – Flower Maiden
> **Hindu Goddess Pavarti** – Feminine Beauty
> **Russian Goddess Vesna** – Spring
> **Tibetan Goddess Sgeg Mo Ma** – Inner
>   and Outer Body Beauty
> **Greek Goddess Dike** – Change Through Justice
> **Japanese Goddess Yaya Zakurai** – Bringer of Spring
> **Greek Goddess Maia** – Dawn of Spring
> **Slavic Goddess Kupala** – Herbs and Vegetation Magick

GODDESS INITIATIONS

Call in (ask for) the following Goddesses to be present with you as you journey with their corresponding seasonal food in the upcoming pages:

Asparagus and **Goddess Vesta**
Pink Grapefruit and **Goddess Inanna**
Blood Orange and **Goddess Athena**
New Potatoes and **Goddess Diana**
Pineapple and **Goddess Pele**
Peas and **Goddess Persephone**

More in-season foods: passionfruit, limes, melons, paw paw, watercress, spring onion, sprouts, zucchini flowers, chilli.

FOOD SACREDNESS IN SPRING

First Month Spring Rising

In this first month of spring, we are still sitting in the slumber of winter and slowly start to emerge from the blanket of the shadow of winter's embrace while we wait for the brightness to appear. Move slowly and gently as you start to head more outdoors to select and shop for foods. Being in large crowds will drain your energy bodies (emotionally, mentally, physically or spiritually), so shop and select foods at times different to others and enjoy home-delivered goods for most of the week.

Cooking at this time still calls for warming meals that take a little time to prepare and cook but we move away from large amounts of rich-flavoured slow cooking and into slightly faster 'wet' meals, quicker roasts and one-pan stovetop-simmered dishes like risotto. Cooking foods together in one pan will support you best at this time of transition, keeping all those nutrients together for maximum taste and wellbeing.

Cooking Methods

Simmering
Food cooked in liquid that gently bubbles away over a low-medium heat source.

Quick Roasts
Cooking suitable foods through a dry heat in a closed environment (oven or hooded barbecue) and at a higher temperature than usual for a shorter cooking time.

Recipes
Quick Roasted Asparagus Tart page 102
Vanilla Simmered Pink Grapefruit page 106

Asparagus and Goddess Vesta

The most enthusiastic of *all* spring vegetables is asparagus—one of the first shooting vegetables of the season and marker that spring has arrived. So, no wonder they wanted to appear first in the book!

With their fast-growing nature and boyish, childlike demeanour, asparagus is one vegetable that does not like to wait and can grow impatient (i.e., will turn fast if stored for too long) if not appreciated by you soon after purchasing. This vegetable is wonderful to purchase direct from a grower at a farmers'/outdoor produce market as you will know that they haven't travelled far and were most likely picked within hours of appearing in front of you too.

Because of their energy and being one of the first spring vegetables to appear for purchase, they really help you to awaken from winter's slumber and will aid in any feelings of sluggishness you hold in your energetic bodies. Get ready to feel rejuvenated.

> **Call in Roman Goddess of the Hearth, Vesta, to align with asparagus for the following:**
> Home + Love + Fertility

Goddess Vesta and asparagus come together to share the message of deep familial love offered when gatherings happen around the hearth at home. Use lavender and garnet crystals to add to your spiritual practice with asparagus and Goddess Vesta.

Plant allies include:
These are the most aligned flavour boosters and partners that support asparagus best when cooking and eating.

> **Herbs:** parsley, tarragon, sage, chives, chervil, basil
> **Spices:** garlic, chillies, mustards
> **Vegetables:** mushrooms, potatoes, dark leafy greens, onions, leeks
> **Fruits:** avocado, tomatoes, oranges, lemons, limes
> **Grains/cereals:** rices, millet, bulgur, couscous, quinoa
> **Beans/legumes:** butter, cannellini, lentils
> **Healthy fats:** olive oils, avocado oil, nuts and seeds
> **Other proteins:** soft and firm tofu, tempeh

Market
Available in green-, purple- or white-coloured spears. Select brightly coloured spears that feel firm when you lightly bend them and have crisp tips that show no signs of being wet (this indicates long periods of storage).

Allow ½-1 bunch per person when serving.

Nurture
If possible, try to prepare, cook and enjoy asparagus on the day of purchase. With its fast-growing nature, they most enjoy a speedy turnaround from when being picked to when being served to you. Otherwise, wrap in kitchen paper towel and then a slightly damp clean tea towel and store in your fridge for up to one day, maximum.

Honour
Lightly snap at the base to remove the woody, fibrous ends and keep them for making vegetable stock. Use spears as they are in full or slice as required. Asparagus desires to be lightly cooked only to retain its fresh taste, with a slight bite. Blanch, steam, chargrill, grill or pan-fry.

Enjoy raw or cooked.

Kitchen helpers
Those young and young at heart find so much joy in bending asparagus ends until they snap.

ASPARAGUS RECIPE

Quick Roasted Asparagus Tart

Serves 4
Preparation 20 minutes
Cooking 15 minutes

1 x frozen sheet puff pastry, at room temperature
2 bunches thin green asparagus, ends trimmed
2 tablespoons extra-virgin olive oil
1 tablespoon finely chopped chives
2 tablespoons chopped, shelled hazelnuts

1. Preheat oven to 220°C fan-forced. Line a large baking tray with non-stick baking paper.
2. Place the sheet of puff pastry onto the prepared tray. Lightly score a 2 cm border around the edge of the pastry, then prick the base all over.
3. Arrange the asparagus in a single layer inside the border of the pastry. Drizzle with the oil, then scatter with the chives and hazelnuts. Roast for 13–15 minutes or until the pastry is puffed and golden and asparagus just tender. Season to taste. Serve warm or at room temperature.

Additions
If you choose to eat dairy, you can sprinkle the tart with crumbled feta or goat's cheese just before serving, if desired.

Serve alongside
A lovely crisp garden salad.

Pink Grapefruit and Goddess Inanna

Pink grapefruit is the slightly less tart, sweeter variety of grapefruit. Available in white-, yellow-, pink- and a deep red-coloured flesh, grapefruit in general is known as a great breakfast fruit that's packed with vitamin C.

The message from pink grapefruit is to view Her as more than a simple snacking fruit. She wishes to be expressed in dishes served as meals whether they are sweet or savoury and served raw or cooked. Embrace versatility beyond the known and currently adopted view of this somewhat polarising fruit in terms of popular opinion.

Grapefruit also like to cluster together, so if choosing to simply serve raw on their own, select a variety of colours to add interest when serving—spring colour palette perfection.

> **Call in Sumerian Great Goddess, Inanna,
> to align with pink grapefruit for the following:**
> Leadership + Protection + Empowerment

Goddess Inanna and pink grapefruit come with the message of love and war, the divine magick of life and the wisdom gained through seeing both life and death as equally empowering. Both symbolise protection for community through their potency. Use reeds turned into rosettes and lapis lazuli crystals to add to your spiritual practice with pink grapefruit and Goddess Inanna.

Plant allies include:
These are the most aligned flavour boosters and partners that support pink grapefruit best when cooking and eating:

> **Herbs:** tarragon, mint, chives, parsley, thyme
> **Spices:** cardamon, vanilla, chillies, paprika, cinnamon, mustards
> **Vegetables:** salad leaves, potatoes, dark leafy greens, onions
> **Fruits:** olives, oranges, lemons, limes, berries
> **Grains/cereals:** rices, couscous, quinoa, freekeh
> **Beans/legumes:** butter, cannellini, lentils, chickpeas, red kidney
> **Healthy fats:** olive oils, avocado oil, nuts and seeds
> **Other proteins:** firm tofu, tempeh

Market
Select heavy-feeling fruit, indicating juiciness, with unblemished skins that are smooth and wrinkle-free with a lovely fragrance.

Allow 1 whole fruit per person when serving.

Nurture
Pink grapefruit will keep at room temperature in your fruit bowl, out of direct sunlight, for up to two weeks or in your fridge for slightly longer.

Honour
You can use the finely grated rind in salad dressings, in marinades or added to baked sweets. The white pith inside is quite thick and exceptionally bitter, so it must be fully

removed before using. Slice, segment or juice. Enjoy raw or cooked.

Kitchen helpers
Pink grapefruit are particularly fun to peel by hand and, with their natural oils being released into the air as you do so, gift you a delicious fragrance that will linger for a few hours.

PINK GRAPEFRUIT RECIPE

Vanilla Simmered Pink Grapefruit

Serves 4
Preparation 20 minutes
Cooking 10 minutes

6 pink grapefruit, peel and pith removed + sliced into rounds
2 vanilla beans, split lengthways + seeds scraped
2 tablespoons pure maple syrup
1 tablespoon thyme leaves
Toasted flaked almonds, to serve

1. Place grapefruit, vanilla seeds and their pods, the syrup and 1 ½ cups (375 ml) water into a large, deep frying pan over a medium heat. Bring the mixture to a simmer, then reduce the heat slightly to a gentle simmer.
2. Simmer, occasionally shaking the pan gently, for 6–8 minutes or until the syrup reduces by half.
3. Remove the pan from heat and sprinkle with the thyme leaves. Serve warm or at room temperature sprinkled with flaked almonds.

Additions
Add a good dollop of your favourite yoghurt of choice before serving.

Serve alongside
Chilled chia pudding or freshly made breakfast crepes.

Second Month Spring Surrender

You'll find an urge to be in public spaces more and will want to immerse all of your senses with spring's new offerings, to really smell and see all of those flowers and produce on display.

Outdoor farmers' or produce markets are the places to be so that you can hand-select fresh produce which will enliven your whole self and really spark that desire to cook in the kitchen.

Open the windows and doors to your kitchen temple space and feel the energy of the fresh spring air circulate around, clearing out the old and bringing in the new. Pluck fresh herbs that you've grown yourself too.

We say a final goodbye to any slow-cooked dishes and quick roasted meals and look towards using more of our stovetops with one-pan dishes still featuring heavily here, even though we'll spend less time preparing and cooking overall.

Cooking Methods

Easy baking
This is to cook food through the use of some type of dry heat, usually an oven. Easy baking is baked items that take minimal time to prepare and cook in the oven, such as quick tarts or pastries, one-bowl cakes, slices or cookies.

Sautéing
Browning foods first at a higher heat with minimal amounts of healthy fats, then reducing heat to low or medium to finish off the cooking.

Recipes
One-Bowl Blood Orange Teacake page 111
Sautéed New Potatoes with Spring Goddess Dressing page 115

Blood Orange and Goddess Athena

Their name would suggest something sinister for sure, but blood orange, once their skins have been removed, are truly one of the most amazing-looking fruits. They have flesh that can shapeshift from full blood red, to those reds and oranges combined or even with a marbling of deep pinky purples. Blood orange wishes to express that looks from the outside can be deceiving and what is offered internally, or what comes from within, is of highest value.

Blood orange definitely holds the energy of nobility and wisdom, able to hold their own in any situation and as such like to be the heroine of any dish.

> **Call in Greek Goddess of Wisdom, Athena, to align with blood orange for the following:**
> Courage + Wisdom + Purity

Goddess Athena and blood orange come together to share with you that having courage is wise and through wisdom we are able to purify our energetic body. Protection can come from outer layers, but the greatest protection comes from within. Use oak or olive leaves and ruby crystals to add to your spiritual practice with blood orange and Goddess Athena.

Plant allies include:
These are the most aligned flavour boosters and partners that support blood orange best when cooking and eating:

> **Herbs:** basil, mint, chives, parsley, thyme
> **Spices:** vanilla, chillies, mustards, ginger, garlic

Vegetables: salad leaves, potatoes, dark leafy greens, onions
Fruits: olives, oranges, lemons, limes
Grains/cereals: rices, couscous, quinoa, freekeh, flours, pastry
Beans/legumes: butter, cannellini, lentils, chickpeas, red kidney
Healthy fats: olive oils, avocado oil, nuts and seeds
Other proteins: firm tofu, tempeh

Market
Select heavy-feeling fruit, indicating juiciness, with unblemished skins that are smooth and wrinkle-free with a lovely fragrance. The skins can either be bright blood red or have a marbled look with orange tones too.

Allow 1 whole fruit per person when serving.

Nurture
Blood orange will keep at room temperature in your fruit bowl, out of direct sunlight, for up to one week or in your fridge for slightly longer.

Honour
You can use the finely grated rind in salad dressings, in marinades or added to baked sweets. Slice, segment or juice. They're wonderful made into marmalade. Enjoy raw or cooked.

Kitchen helpers
Those young and young at heart find so much joy juicing the halved fresh fruit to see the varying shades of orange to deep blood red colours that appear.

BLOOD ORANGE RECIPE

One-Bowl Blood Orange Teacake

Serves 4
Preparation 20 minutes + 5 minutes cooling
Cooking 30 minutes

70 g dairy-free spread
½ cup caster sugar, plus 3 extra teaspoons
¼ cup apple puree
1 teaspoon vanilla bean paste
1 cup self-raising flour
¼ cup (60ml) oat milk
2 blood orange, peel and pith removed + sliced into rounds

1. Preheat oven to 180°C/160°C fan-forced. Line the base and side of a 20 cm round cake pan with non-stick baking paper.
2. Place the spread and sugar in a bowl and beat together using an electric hand-mixer for 3 minutes on high until light and fluffy. Add puree and paste, beat until just combined. Add flour and milk, beat until just combined. Spoon batter into prepared pan, level surface and then arrange the blood orange slices on top, in a single layer but overlapping slightly. Sprinkle top with extra sugar.
3. Bake for 25–30 minutes or until cooked when a skewer inserted at centre comes out clean. Cool in pan for 5 minutes before transferring to a wire rack to cool slightly. Serve warm or at room temperature.

Additions
Add ½ teaspoon of ground cardamom to the extra caster sugar before sprinkling over the top of the blood oranges before baking.

Serve alongside
Your favourite cup of hot herbal tea.

New Potatoes and Goddess Diana

New potatoes are such as they're the first to appear of the potato family, with their sweetness coming from a lack of maturity through their starch.

These paper-thin skinned potatoes may seem fragile on the outside but hold great strength through their waxy texture inside, and because of this hold their shape after cooking.

With their delicious taste and flexibility in cooking style, new potatoes can independently stand on their own without too many additional flavours needing to be added. A simple drizzle of extra-virgin olive oil and some sea salt flakes and freshly ground pepper is all that they really need—easily and joyfully ready for the world!

> **Call in Roman Queen Goddess of the Hunt and Moon, Diana,
> to align with new potatoes for the following:**
> Independence + Strength + Cycles

Goddess Diana and new potatoes offer you the message of cycles and trusting that in each cycle what will be revealed is meant to, plus that there is great strength found in humbleness. Diana was also known as Goddess of humbleness and potatoes, well, the original humble vegie that can gift us their presence at any seasonal cycle of the year. Use jasmine and moonstone crystals to add to your spiritual practice with new potatoes and Goddess Diana.

Plant allies include:
These are the most aligned flavour boosters and partners that support new potatoes best when cooking and eating:

> **Herbs:** rosemary, parsley, tarragon, sage, chives, chervil, basil, coriander, oregano
> **Spices:** garlic, chillies, mustards, saffron, paprika, curry powders
> **Vegetables:** dark leafy greens, mushrooms, root vegetables, dark leafy greens, onions
> **Fruits:** tomatoes, lemons
> **Grains/Cereals:** flours, pastry
> **Beans/Legumes:** red kidney
> **Healthy fats:** olive oils, avocado oil, macadamia oil, nuts and seeds

Market
Select new potatoes that look fresh with crisp, dry, flaky-thin skins still attached. The skins may have a pink hue to them also. The flesh underneath can be creamy-pale yellow, to slightly darker shades of yellow or even look as though they're pink. There shouldn't be any dark patches or visible blemishes either.

Allow approximately 200 g per person, before cooking.

Nurture
Keep purchased new potatoes in a dark, cool, dry and well-ventilated space for up to three days, maximum.

Honour
A little, light wipe over from a slightly damp tea towel is all that is needed in terms of preparation, but don't rub too hard or the skins will peel away. New potatoes ask for you to leave their skins on, as they are delightfully edible.

Boil, steam, pan-fry or roast whole or halved.

Kitchen helpers
Allow a young helper to carefully wipe over the new potatoes for you.

NEW POTATO RECIPE

Sautéed New Potatoes with Spring Goddess Dressing

Serves 4
Preparation 15 minutes
Cooking 15 minutes

¼ cup (60 ml) avocado oil
800 g small new potatoes, halved

Spring Goddess Dressing
1 small clove garlic
1 cup basil leaves
2 tablespoons chopped chives
½ cup tarragon leaves
¼ cup (60 ml) red wine vinegar

1. Make the *Spring Goddess Dressing* first, by placing all the ingredients together in a food processor and processing until almost smooth. Set aside.
2. Heat the oil in a large deep-frying pan over a medium heat. Add potatoes and cook, tossing occasionally for 12–15 minutes or until tender and golden crisp.
3. Remove the pan from the heat and immediately add the *Spring Goddess Dressing*, tossing to coat well. Season to taste. Serve warm or at room temperature.

   Additions
   You can add 1 thickly sliced onion to the pan along with the potatoes, if desired, and/or toss through a few handfuls of baby spinach leaves at the end to just wilt slightly.

   Serve alongside
   Your favourite chargrilled protein of choice, such as firm tofu steaks, chicken breast or minute steaks.

Third Month Spring Emerging

We feel the energy rising through the longer days that start to appear and the weather warming up as we emerge from spring. We're adding more sweet foods to what we cook at this time (adding sweet fruits to salad vegetables) and using quick styles of cookery for food elements to be added into dishes, like the addition of toasted nuts in salads or sprinkled over steamed vegetables. We naturally want to be spending more time outside, but not quite ready to cook completely outside yet, so we use stovetop chargrill pans for that 'taste' of summer that's on the horizon. Dishes that are easily transportable feature greatly here as we can take them along to gatherings with loved ones as we commune outside more at picnics or community fares.

Cooking Methods

Steaming
Food cooked in an elevated container, usually perforated, and away from a direct heat source. The steam is generated by boiling liquids from underneath which then rises to cook the food.

Stovetop chargrilling
Using a flat-sided or lipped pan with ridges that is preheated over a stovetop on a very high heat for faster cooking.

Shallow frying
Items like zucchini fritters, leftover vegetable hash browns, lightly coated onion rings or homemade falafel.

Recipes
Chargrilled Pineapple with Mint Limes page 120
Steamed Pea and Lentil Toss page 124

Pineapple and Goddess Pele

Pineapple—the sweet seductress would have you believe, simply based on Her looks and prickly exterior, that what lies beneath it all would not be worth the effort that preparing Her takes.

Intoxicatingly moreish, pineapple expresses Her joy when shared in gatherings at your home with family and friends. She is one for being on display and at the centre of the fruit bowl. Pineapple thoroughly enjoys having *all* of her served up.

Try cutting in half lengthways, placing onto a serving platter cut side-facing up and then simply score the flesh inside into sections, allowing your guests to spoon out what they desire.

She is a true Queen, crown and all.

> **Call in Hawaiian Volcano Goddess, Pele,
> to align with pineapple for the following:**
> Creativity + Seduction + Harmony

Goddess Pele and pineapple come together, offering you sweet harmony for inspiration. The hot, steaming chargrilled pineapple will activate Her energy and invoke your own inner fire. Use frangipani and lava rocks or black obsidian crystals to add to your spiritual practice with pineapple and Goddess Pele.

Plant allies include:
These are the most aligned flavour boosters and partners that support pineapple best when cooking and eating:

> **Herbs:** mint, basil, coriander
> **Spices:** ginger, chillies, vanilla
> **Vegetables:** green onions
> **Fruits:** tomatoes, banana, berries, lemons, limes, avocado, all tropical fruits
> **Grains/cereals:** rices, quinoa, couscous
> **Healthy fats:** nuts and seeds

Market
Your greatest sense here is smell; pick up pineapples and smell for that super sweet aroma. Another guide is to gently pull away a leaf from the centre of the crown and if it slips out easily, it can indicate a lovely ripe fruit.

Allow ¼ small pineapple per person when serving.

Nurture
Store the whole fruit at room temperature in your fruit bowl for up to one day only. Otherwise, wrap in a clean tea towel, leaves left uncovered and store in your fridge for up to two days, maximum. Bring back to room temperature before serving.

Honour
Cut away the base and top, then stand upright and carefully cut away the thick skin, removing the dark-coloured 'eyes' as you go. Slice or cut as required, removing and discarding the fibrous central core as you go. Perfect just as is or grilled, chargrilled, pan-fried or barbecued. Enjoy raw or cooked.

Kitchen helpers
Hand over a small teaspoon to any onlooker and get them to dig out those pesky dark 'eyes' from the fruit.

PINEAPPLE RECIPE

Chargrilled Pineapple and Mint Limes

Serves 4
Preparation 15 minutes
Cooking 5 minutes

1 small whole pineapple, peeled + cut lengthwise into 8
2 limes, halved
¼ cup finely chopped mint
Vanilla coconut yoghurt, to serve

1. Preheat a large chargrill pan over a high heat on your stovetop.
2. Add the pineapple and limes, cut sides facing down. Chargrill for 5 minutes, turning occasionally, until just warmed through and dark golden char lines appear.
3. Divide pineapple among serving plates. Dip the cut sides of the limes into the chopped mint, then serve alongside the pineapple with the yoghurt.

Additions
You can also add chopped basil to the mint for coating the chargrilled limes.

Serve alongside
A lovely macadamia cookie for added crunch.

Peas and Goddess Persephone

Peas are one of the oldest varieties of vegetables that have graced Mother Earth and yet they hold the pure energy of the Maiden in springtime, divinely balanced in energy and physically.

While you can purchase peas frozen all year around there is nothing quite like the taste and texture of a freshly podded pea when in season. This is how peas wish to come to you, as they are inside their pods, for you snap open yourself. Always purchase way more pea pods than what you think you need to, because once you start shelling them, you'll find it exceptionally hard to resist not eating them all!

With their balanced embodied energy, peas enjoy being devoured raw or cooked and lightly cooked is best to retain their sweet freshness and a bit of bite. Once shelled, peas absolutely love to be on display, the heroine of the dish; it's as if they're saying, *Here I am!* while taking a bow. So have an abundance of them at the ready for any dish you are preparing.

> **Call in Greek Maiden Goddess of Spring, Persephone, to align with peas for the following:**
> Innocence + Purity + Wisdom

Goddess Persephone and pea offer you the purity of innocence through youth and also the wisdom gained through life over many years. In this case those years are the longevity of the pea through agriculture. Use any spring flowers and clear quartz crystals to add to your spiritual practice with peas and Goddess Persephone.

Plant allies include:
These are the most aligned flavour boosters and partners that support pea best when cooking and eating:

> **Herbs:** mint, dill, parsley, basil, sage, chervil
> **Spices:** garlic, ginger
> **Vegetables:** dark leafy greens, onions, asparagus, carrot, potatoes, celery, leeks, iceberg lettuce
> **Fruits:** avocado, tomatoes, lemons, limes
> **Grains/cereals:** rices, pasta, breads, pastries
> **Beans/legumes:** lentils, chickpeas
> **Healthy fats:** olive oils, avocado oil, nuts and seeds
> **Other proteins:** firm tofu, tempeh

Market
Select brightly coloured firm pods that look full i.e., that they have well-shaped peas inside. If possible, purchase straight from a grower as they start to lose sweetness within hours of being picked fresh.

Allow 2 handfuls of pods per person, before shelling.

Nurture
Purchase, prepare, lightly cook and enjoy peas on the day of harvesting. With their sensitive sweetness peas really want to be used and eaten as close to their time of picking as possible. If you must store them, do so in an airtight container layered between sheets of kitchen paper towel

in your fridge but do this for as minimal time as possible, absolute maximum one day. They're a pushy little vegie!

Honour
The easiest way to pod peas I've found is to run the tip of your nail down its middle, lengthwise, for it to instantly pop. Their delicateness suits delicate cookery too. Add them into dishes once they have been removed from a heart source, allowing residual heat to warm them through gently. Steaming and blanching are wonderful alternatives. Enjoy raw or cooked.

Kitchen helpers
Many hands make light work for pea podding, gathering those around you who you can trust not to eat too many of the freshly shelled peas. Otherwise set yourself up outside and use the podding time as an active meditation opportunity.

PEA RECIPE

Steamed Pea and Lentil Toss

Serves 4
Preparation 30 minutes
Cooking 5 minutes

2 tablespoons avocado oil
2 tablespoons white wine vinegar
1 small clove garlic, crushed
1 red onion, very thinly sliced
2 x 400 g cans lentils, drained, well rinsed + drained again
Handful fresh herbs, torn (sage, flat-leaf parsley + dill)
800 g pea pods, shelled

1. Combine the oil, vinegar, garlic, onion, lentils and herbs in a large heatproof bowl. Set aside.
2. Add the peas to a steaming basket set over a saucepan of boiling water. Steam for 3–5 minutes or until just tender and bright green.
3. Immediately add the hot peas to the lentil mixture in the bowl, tossing well to combine. Season to taste. Serve warm or at room temperature.

Additions
If you choose to eat dairy, pull apart baby bocconcini and add to the lentil toss before serving.

Serve alongside
Some crisp baby rocket leaves.

SUMMER

Summer Food and Goddess Initiations

Summer Is...
Stepping out fully as your truest self. This is your individual time to shine brightly; cultivate confidence and strength within self and while in groups with others; empowerment through inner radiance; feel the abundance of energy received from the sun's rays and many hours spent outside physically connecting to our great Mother Earth through swimming, hiking or resting on Her lands; stargaze through the long evenings; socialise and make deep community connections.

Sacred feminine energy for summer is the Mother: the becoming of you in your entirety as the compassionate nurturer—the ultimate protector who shows strength through resilience.

> **Summer Magick**
> **Moon cycle is** Full Moon
> **Element is** Fire
> **Direction is** North in Southern Hemisphere / South in Northern Hemisphere
> **Time of day is** High Noon
> **Tools are** Energy and Candles
> **Colours are** Yellows, Ocean and Sky Blues, Pale Greens and Gold

Kitchen Craft for Summer
Start to view your kitchen, the heart and soul of your home, as one big altar. The one sacred, temple space where you and your loved ones can commune together. Try these kitchen (altar) crafts throughout summer:

Bring the abundance of greenery that is visible everywhere from outside, in. Decorate tabletops, or places where you will enjoy meals, with hand-collected leaves and flowers from around where you reside.

Add a selection of candles, with gold ribbons tied around them, and golden crystals such as citrine, sunstone, garnet and tiger's eye to your kitchen windowsill. Light the candles once the sun goes down to continue the sun's light and energy indoors.

Empowering Words
You can speak these words out loud, write them down in your journal or post them up on your fridge for added personal empowerment through summertime. Try these to start you off, then have a go at writing your own too.

> *I radiate inner strength.*
> *I'm ready to be seen in the world.*
> *My passion projects come to life.*

Summer Seasoning: Refreshing Sugar
This is the dedicated seasoning blend for summer and can be used to sweeten herbal teas whether served warm or chilled or sprinkled over freshly cut fruits of the season, toast or Bircher muesli.

Make the vanilla sugar component of this seasoning in one large batch and one week before the first day of summer starts. Store in an airtight container in your dry-store cupboard for the duration of the summer months. Whatever is not used by the end of summer, simply use in your first-baked sweet items made in autumn. There is no need to discard. It's essential to have fresh mint on hand for summer seasoning; having a pot growing by your kitchen is best.

Split 1 vanilla bean in half, lengthwise, and then combine with 1 cup of white granulated sugar in the storage container you will be using. Attach the lid, then shake vigorously using one hand at a time for 30 counts each. Store as mentioned above before using.

For each portion and just before using, place 4 torn mint leaves into a mortar and pestle. Pound until finely crushed, then add 1 tablespoon of the vanilla sugar and stir to combine. Use immediately.

> Each portion makes approx. 1 ½ tablespoons (Serves 1–2 people).
> Vanilla sugar makes 1 cup.

Overarching Goddess Dedication: Slavic Goddess Mokosh
Goddess Mokosh was a surprise to me when She came through for the months of summer, as I was very new to knowing Her. She holds the energy of a loving Mother, the matriarch of the family, one who enjoys deep embraces and reminds me of the loving hugs my Baba would give us. Her embodied elemental energies of earth and water are a natural fit to wanting to be outdoors in this season. She

really invoked within me such a great desire to entertain and cook for others in gathered celebrations, especially outside at our home. I found a new love for raw red cabbage salads with toasted nuts at this time.

More Summer Goddesses
Hawaiian Goddess HAUMEA – abundant mother
Celtic Goddess DRUANTIA – eternally wise mother
Slavic Goddess MATI-SYRA-ZEMLYA
   – abundant Earth Mother
Egyptian Goddess BAST – sunsets
Lybian Goddess MEDUSA – serpent energy
Arabian Goddess AL-LAT – supreme Earth Mother
Welsh Goddess OLWEN – sun and flowers
Maori Goddess MAHUIKA – wildfires

GODDESS INITIATIONS

Call in (ask for) the following Goddesses to be present with you as you journey with their corresponding seasonal food in the upcoming pages:

Peach and **Goddess Kuan Yin**
Tomato and **Goddess Abundantia**
Eggplant and **Goddess Nammu**
Mango and **Goddess Sol**
Blueberry and **Goddess Artemis**
Mushroom and **Goddess Aine**

More in-season foods: cherry, apricots, plum, capsicum, celery, lettuce, onion, radish, corn, zucchini.

FOOD SACREDNESS IN SUMMER

First Month Summer Rising

There is a definite burst of energy in the first month of summer. Everyone is eager to be outside, socialising to their fullest, and there really is an energetic buzz in the air. As our calendars fill with gatherings, we start to pare back how long we prepare and cook foods. Much shorter cooking times, simpler preparations of foods and fresh-tasting meals are at the forefront as we start to 'warm' up into the season. Blanching and braising foods still gives us the connection to our kitchens that we desire, but certainly not labour-intensive. We are excited to receive the abundance of the new season's fresh produce too, especially all of those sweet summer fruits.

Cooking Methods

Blanching
Blanching is quickly plunging vegetables or fruit into large pots of rapidly boiling water for a few seconds to quickly cook. The food is then immediately drained and refreshed either under cold-running tap water or placed into a bowl of iced water to stop the cooking process altogether so that the food remains crisp in texture and brightly coloured.

Braising
Braising uses two cookery methods, starting with browning foods at a higher temperature using small amounts of healthy fats to sear and seal over a stovetop heat. Then liquid is added, the cooking temperature is reduced to very

low and the dish is covered and allowed to simmer very slowly for longer periods of time either on the stovetop or in a medium-temperature oven until the foods are very softened and the liquid thickened slightly by reduction.

Recipes
Blanched Peaches with Oolong Tea Syrup page 135
Braised Tomatoes for Simple Pasta page 139

Peach and Goddess Kuan Yin

Cheeky, cheeky peach. All you need to do is take a good look at the shape of these little beauties to see exactly what their true personalities are.

Peaches carry the energy of abundance and luck. They have throughout time been honoured as a fruit that can offer you longevity, steeped historically in maiden rites of passage and honouring the sacred, fertile feminine. They truly wish to invoke within you that youthful, joyful, playful fun while you enjoy eating them.

> **Call in Chinese Goddess of Mercy, Kuan Yin,
> to align with peach for the following:**
> Fertility + Compassion + Immortality

Goddess Kuan Yin and peach offer you the message of compassion and that when we can view all of life through the combination of using our heart space with a maiden energy, we literally bring to life the abundance we desire.

Use lotus flowers and jade crystals to add to your spiritual practice with peach and Goddess Kuan Yin.

Plant allies include:
These are the most aligned flavour boosters and partners that support peach best when cooking and eating:

> **Herbs:** parsley, tarragon, sage, chives, chervil, basil, mint
> **Spices:** vanilla, ginger, nutmeg, cinnamon
> **Vegetables:** dark leafy greens, green onions
> **Fruits:** all citrus, other stone fruits, berries
> **Grains/cereals:** rices, couscous, quinoa, flours, pastries
> **Beans/legumes:** cannellini, lentils
> **Healthy fats:** olive oils, avocado oil, nuts and seeds
> **Other proteins:** firm tofu, tempeh

Market
Ripeness will be indicated by their skin colour, aroma and how they feel when you hold them gently in your hands. Do not squeeze them though, peaches like a gentle touch as they bruise easily. Always check that the fruit are free from cracked skins, soft patches and bruising through rough handling.

Allow ½–1 fruit per person when serving.

Nurture
Peaches can be kept in your fruit bowl at room temperature, but out of direct sunlight, for up to two–three days. Ripe peaches should be enjoyed between one–two days after

bringing home and to prolong their softening, store in your fridge for up to two days. Bring back to room temperature before enjoying.

Honour
Using a small sharp knife, run it around the circumference of the fruit making sure to cut all the way down to the pit. Twist to open up in half and then either pick out the pit or cut around it (this will ease the pit being removed, depending on the variety and ripeness). Enjoy raw or cooked.

Kitchen helpers
Those young and young at heart find so much joy in pulling out those internal peach pits.

PEACH RECIPE

Blanched Peach with Oolong Tea Syrup

Serves 4
Preparation 20 minutes
Cooking 10 minutes

4 firm, ripe peaches
2 cups (500 ml) brewed oolong tea
2 star anise
2 cinnamon sticks, broken in half
½ cup coconut sugar

1. Lightly score a cross at both ends of each peach. Bring a large saucepan of water to the boil over a high heat, then plunge the peaches in and cook for 30 seconds only. Remove immediately to a bowl of iced water, set aside.
2. Place the brewed tea, spices and sugar in a saucepan over a high heat and bring to the boil, stirring constantly. Boil, untouched, for 10 minutes or until reduced by a third and thickened slightly. Set aside.
3. Carefully peel and discard the skins of the peaches, then place into small serving bowls. Pour over the warm tea syrup. Serve.

Additions
Add a few bruised cardamom pods to the tea syrup when boiling.

Serve alongside
Top with a crumbling of meringue and dollop of your cream of choice.

Tomato and Goddess Abundantia

Tomatoes rejoice in being the epitome of abundance energy as a summer fruit crop gathering together in large numbers, just waiting to be eaten, used in cooking or preserved and stored at a later date.

Their varieties and uses are as abundant as their energetic vibe. They're one of the only fruits I've come across who really, strongly want you to grow them at home for absolute enjoyment, especially as when left to ripen fully on their trees will give you a sensational-tasting tomato.

Tomatoes love the community aspect they can invoke in us all through gatherings around preparing them (i.e., making passata) and feasts where shared plates are served.

> **Call in Roman Goddess of Good Fortune, Abundantia,**
> **to align with tomato for the following:**
> Success + Prosperity + Protection

Goddess Abundantia and tomato when combined together create immense abundance in terms of great protection in your health and bringing good fortune into your home. Use peonies and pyrite crystals to add to your spiritual practice with tomato and Goddess Abuntantia.

Plant allies include:
These are the most aligned flavour boosters and partners that support tomato best when cooking and eating:

Herbs: parsley, tarragon, sage, chives, basil, oregano
Spices: garlic, chillies, mustards, dried basil, thyme, oregano, paprika
Vegetables: all salad vegetables and leaves, mushrooms, all root vegetables, dark leafy greens, onions
Fruits: avocado, lemons, limes
Grains/cereals: pastas, breads, rices, couscous, quinoa, polenta
Beans/legumes: all varieties
Healthy fats: olive oils, avocado oil, nuts and seeds
Other proteins: firm tofu, tempeh

Market
If wanting to enjoy tomatoes on the same day as selection, then choose brightly coloured ones that give a little when gently held in your hand. Otherwise select a range of tomatoes that are slightly green all the way through to red— that way you can use some straight away and leave others out to enjoy for later in the week.

Allow one per person when serving.

Nurture
Tomatoes really don't like to be chilled, so always leave them out on your kitchen countertop and enjoy at room temperature. All store-bought tomatoes will require some 'sunbaking' time on your windowsill to help ripen further and deepen their flavour. Already purchased ripe tomatoes should be eaten between one–two days and those that come home green will need a good five–seven days in sunlight before being ready.

Honour
Simply remove the top core of the tomato, lightly rinse under running tap water, wipe dry and use as directed in the recipe you're using. Enjoy raw, cooked or preserved.

Kitchen helpers
Many hands make light work in the kitchen if you choose to blanch and remove the skins from tomato. Follow the steps as shown in the peach recipe share on page 135 and once the tomatoes are chilled in the cold water, hand them over to others to peel and discard the skins for you.

*This recipe can easily be doubled, tripled or quadrupled (just so long as you have enough large saucepans for cooking) to feed as many people as you desire, in true abundance!

TOMATO RECIPE

Braised Tomatoes for Simple Pasta

Serves 4
Preparation 15 minutes
Cooking 20 minutes

¼ cup (60 ml) extra-virgin olive oil
2 cloves garlic, crushed
8 very ripe tomatoes, chopped
2 tablespoon tomato paste
½ cup (125 ml) white wine
Handful basil leaves
500 g packet spaghetti

1. Heat the oil in a large, deep frying pan over a medium heat. Add the garlic and tomatoes. Cook, stirring occasionally, for 3 minutes or until they are starting to collapse and stick to the base of the pan slightly. Add the tomato paste. Cook, stirring constantly, for 1 minute. Add wine and basil, stir well, then reduce heat slightly to a gentle simmer. Simmer for 15 minutes or until the sauce reduces by half again. Season to taste.
2. Meanwhile, cook the spaghetti in a large saucepan of boiling water for 8–10 minutes or until just tender. Drain, reserving ½ cup of the cooking water.
3. Return the spaghetti to the pan, off the heat, and add the tomato mixture and just enough of the reserved cooking water to form a lovely coating on the pasta. Season to taste again, then serve.

Additions
Add a small handful of pitted green olives to the pasta just before serving.

Serve alongside
A crisp Italian-leaf salad dressed with balsamic and extra-virgin olive oil.

Second Month Summer Surrender

We welcome in the height of the heat of the summer sun and as we gather in celebrations outdoors, we do this slowly so that we can last through the long days and into the evenings conserving our energy. We take everything outside now and the majority of the cooking is through barbecuing. We go to eat out in establishments more and when we are inside at home we snack on simple, sweet, refreshing foods that are mostly raw rather than big meals. We also plan and prepare foods in the morning or the night before for the day ahead by either marinating or maceration. This makes cooking at lunchtimes or late afternoons just that much easier. The emphasis is on keeping cooler, so you'll find yourself shopping very early in the mornings to select foods and often do multiple shops throughout the week rather than one larger one.

Cooking Methods

Barbecue
Cooking outdoors over an open, high-heat flame using either a grill-plate or flat-plate for the foods to rest on.

Macerate
Immerging foods in plain or flavoured liquids to soften them.

Recipes
Barbecued Marinated Eggplant and Smashed Hummus page 144
Macerated Mango and Caramelised Macadamias page 148

Eggplant and Goddess Nammu

Multifaceted is a word that doesn't even come close to explaining how versatile this vegetable (that is actually a berry) is, and the many varieties that are available too. Worldwide, eggplants are known in many cuisines as the feature ingredient and they pride themselves on being a great nourisher to all.

In this instance, the eggplant wishing to come forward is the medium-sized dark, purple-skinned variety that is readily available to us. She mimics the feminine form, with a large curvy base. Eggplants hold the essence of transformation.

They can be used in many ways and elevated from their humble, neural taste to something extraordinary by adding additional flavours. With such a thick flesh, eggplant is an amazing plant-food alternative to any meat in dishes and can withstand being baked, fried or grilled.

> **Call in Summerian Mother Goddess of Creation, Nammu, to align with eggplant for the following:**
> Creation + Abundance + Nurturing

Goddess Nammu and eggplant bring forward the energy of the handmaiden. They offer you deep nourishment in however you wish for them to be of service to you, in whichever way you desire to create with them for the deepest nourishment of self.

Use hydrangea and tangerine quartz crystals to add to your spiritual practice with eggplant and Goddess Nammu.

Plant allies include:
These are the most aligned flavour boosters and partners that support eggplant best when cooking and eating:

> **Herbs:** parsley, tarragon, sage, chives, oregano, basil, thyme, coriander, mint
> **Spices:** garlic, chillies, mustards, ginger, cumin, coriander, peppers
> **Vegetables:** mushrooms, all root vegetables, dark leafy greens, onions
> **Fruits:** tomatoes, avocado, all citrus
> **Grains/cereals:** pastas, rices, millet, bulgur, couscous, quinoa, flours, pastries, freekeh
> **Beans/legumes:** all varieties
> **Healthy fats:** olive oils, avocado oil, macadamia oil, nuts and seeds
> **Other proteins:** soft and firm tofu, tempeh

Market
Select eggplant that have a very shiny skin, feel firm and heavy for their size and are blemish-free.

Allow ½ medium-sized per person when serving.

Nurture
You can store eggplant in a large brown paper bag, whole, in your fridge for up to one week. Be careful of their tip as it holds sharpness and will prick your finger easily if handled incorrectly. You can use eggplant straight from the fridge too—no need to bring to room temperature. Give a good wipe over with a damp clean tea towel, washing isn't recommended.

Honour
As mentioned above eggplants can be used in a variety of different ways. Simply top and tail their ends before preparing as directed through any recipe shared. Their skins are completely edible, so no need to peel before using either. Enjoy cooked.

Kitchen helpers
Gather whomever you can to help score the flesh of eggplants for you.

EGGPLANT RECIPE

Barbecued Marinated Eggplant and Smashed Hummus

Serves 4
Preparation 10 minutes + 4 hours marinating time
Cooking 10 minutes

2 medium eggplant, halved lengthways + flesh scored
2 cloves garlic, sliced
1 long red chilli, chopped
⅓ cup (80 ml) extra-virgin olive oil
1 x 400 g can chickpeas, drained, well rinsed + drained again
1 tablespoon tahini
2 lemons, rind finely grated + juiced

1. Place the eggplants, cut sides facing up in a glass dish, side by side. Fill the scored sections with the garlic slices and chilli, then drizzle with half the oil. Season to taste. Cover and chill for at least 4 hours to marinate.
2. Preheat a barbecue chargrill plate to medium-high. Place the chickpeas, tahini, lemon rind and juice and the remaining oil together in a bowl, then mash together until roughly smooth. Season to taste. Set aside.
3. Chargrill the eggplant for 3–4 minutes each side or until tender and dark golden. Transfer to a serving platter, spoon over the chickpea mixture. Serve warm.

Additions
Add some finely chopped flat-leaf parsley or chives to the chickpea mixture before serving.

Serve alongside
Other barbecued seasonal vegetables and crisp salad greens.

Mango and Goddess Sol

Mango = summer! Particularly summers spent by the beach. With their golden flesh that looks like the sun herself, mangoes pride themselves on being a perfect little package of sweetness.

Tranquillity and stillness are the message that comes from mango as they consider themselves to be the only fruit that can truly enrich and nourish your meditation practice after completion.

> **Call in Norse Goddess of the Sun, Sol, to align with mango for the following:**
> Blessings + Movement + Inspiration

Goddess Sol and mango want to share the immense gloriousness you can receive from spending some quiet, slow-moving hours outside during summertime; you can literally be inspired by the beauty of what the sun shines down onto. Use sunflowers and amber crystals to add to your spiritual practice with mango and Goddess Sol.

Plant allies include:
These are the most aligned flavour boosters and partners that support mango best when cooking and eating:

> **Herbs:** parsley, chives, mint, basil,
> **Spices:** garlic, chillies, ginger
> **Vegetables:** salad greens, dark leafy greens, onions, celery

Fruits: tomatoes, oranges, lemons, limes, all tropical fruits
Grains/cereals: rices, couscous, quinoa, flours, pastry
Beans/legumes: red kidney beans
Healthy fats: olive oils, avocado oil, macadamia oil, nuts and seeds
Other proteins: firm tofu, tempeh

Market
The intoxicating aroma of a mango will indicate to you which fruit to choose as the skins can vary in colours from orange to creamy pinks, greens and reds, depending on their variety. Be sure to select fruit that don't have any dark blemishes on them.

Allow 1 small whole fruit or ½ a large per person when serving.

Nurture
Mangoes love to be served at room temperature so that you can really taste their sweetness. If you bring home already ripe fruit, enjoy it within one day or store in your fridge for up to three days, maximum. If the fruit is unripe on purchasing, leave out in your fruit bowl for three–five days.

Honour
Mangoes have a thin, fibrous large seed at their centres. Use a large, sharp knife to slice their 'cheeks' away from the seed before using the tip of a smaller knife to score the flesh. Turn inside out and eat the porcupine-looking pieces as is, or grab a large spoon and simply scoop out the mango pieces away from the skins. Alternatively, you can peel the skins

away first, then remove the cheeks which then offers you the opportunity on slicing the flesh into strips. Enjoy raw.

Kitchen helpers
After removing the 'cheeks' from their seeds, and then scoring the flesh that is still held within those skins, hand over a dessert spoon for someone nearby to scoop the scored pieces out for you into a bowl.

MANGO RECIPE

Macerated Mango and Caramelised Macadamia

Serves 4
Preparation 15 minutes + 30 minutes maceration time
Cooking 5 minutes

4 mangoes, peeled + flesh thinly sliced
2 limes, rind finely grated + juiced
1 teaspoon freshly grated ginger
1 cup raw macadamia halves
2 tablespoons pure maple syrup

1. Place the mango, ginger, lime rind and juice in a bowl. Stir gently to combine, cover with a clean tea towel. Set aside in a cool place for at least 30 minutes to macerate, stirring gently occasionally.
2. Place the macadamia and syrup together in a large, non-stick frying pan over a medium-high heat. Cook, stirring constantly, for 2–3 minutes or until dark golden. Remove pan from heat.
3. Divide the mango between flat serving bowls and spoon over the warm macadamias. Serve.

Additions
You may wish to do a mixture of nuts and seeds.

Serve alongside
A scoop of your favourite summertime granita.

Third Month Summer Emerging

While the summer sun still engulf us at this turn in the season, we start to long for a cooler change. Really fast-cooking methods like stir-frying make their peak entrance at this time and raw foods are the main heroines. We start to slow down with all the outside socialising, bringing it back home for more balance and we look forward to enjoying meals with just those closest and dearest to us. We use an abundance of brightly coloured foods at mealtimes to match the vibrancy of the weather. Cooling iced treats late in the evenings as you watch the sun go down are the perfect antidote to a hot summer's day.

Cooking Methods

Raw
Foods not heated or cooked above 46–47.5°C / 115–118°F.

Stir-fry
Rapidly cook foods over a very high heat, while tossing or stirring briskly for minimal amounts of time.

Recipes
Raw Blueberry Mousse page 152
Stir-Fry Ginger Mushrooms with Udon page 156

Other cookery ideas for summer and Freezer sweets
Granitas, nice-creams, parfaits, iced-pops or freezer fudges are great sweet treats to have in your freezer throughout summer as go-to refreshers during hot days and for a mid-afternoon energy boost too.

Blueberry and Goddess Artemis

Blueberries *love* gatherings; they love to be together in a group and symbolise the energy of a bunch of young children playing.

With their antioxidants and delicious blue hue, blueberries offer immense amounts of healing. Simply grabbing handfuls of them to enjoy is how best to devour them. Blueberries are the original 'star children' of Mother Earth and you can see this by turning them around to see their five-pointed star imprint in their skins and also due to their love for growing together in 'clusters'.

> **Call in Greek Goddess of the Wilderness, Artemis, to align with blueberry for the following:**
> Focus + Protection + Wildness

Goddess Artemis and blueberry join together as a collective, wild force of protection—Artemis yielding Her sacred bow and arrow and blueberries with their star imprint 'eyes'. Use amaranth flowers and amethyst crystals to add to your spiritual practice with blueberry and Goddess Artemis.

Plant allies include:
These are the most aligned flavour boosters and partners that support blueberry best when cooking and eating:

> **Herbs:** mint, basil
> **Spices:** vanilla, ginger, nutmeg, cinnamon, lemon myrtle
> **Fruits:** avocado, all citrus, all tropical fruits

Grains/cereals: rices, couscous, quinoa, flours, pastries
Healthy fats: nuts and seeds

Market
Check carefully over the punnets of blueberries to make sure none of them are either soft or have crinkly skins. Blueberries should appear firm and brightly coloured.

Allow ½ punnet per person when serving.

Nurture
If the blueberries appear dusty, simply wipe them over with a slightly damp piece of kitchen paper towel. They'll never really need washing. Enjoy as close to purchasing as possible, but they can be kept in their punnets in your fridge for up to one week.

Honour
The beauty of blueberries lies in their true simplicity; you don't need to do anything with them in preparation of either eating straight up as they are, or if you decide to cook with them in jams, sauces or other sweet treats. Enjoy raw or cooked in sweet dishes.

Kitchen helpers
No help is required with these lovelies, but watch those hands as the blueberries will disappear quickly if left unattended (they do in our house anyway)!

BLUEBERRY RECIPE

Raw Blueberry Mousse

Serves 4
Preparation 15 minutes
Chilling 1 hour

2 large avocados, flesh scooped out
⅓ cup cocoa powder
⅓ cup (80 ml) pure maple syrup
2 teaspoons vanilla bean paste
1 cup (250 ml) thick coconut cream
2 x punnets blueberries

1. Place the avocado flesh, cocoa, syrup, paste and cream together in an upright, high-speed blender. Blend until completely smooth and aerated—the mixture will be slightly lighter in colour and resemble a chocolate mousse.
2. Divide the mousse mixture between serving glasses, layering as you go with the blueberries. Chill for at least 1 hour.
3. Serve chilled.

Additions
Top the chilled blueberry mousse with toasted flaked coconut.

Serve alongside
Almond biscotti for dipping into the mousse.

Mushroom and Goddess Aine

If you've ever grown mushrooms at home, you will agree wholeheartedly with me about their magickal abilities. All of a sudden overnight they simply appear out of the soil; you harvest and then again, they continue to keep producing volumes for you that you can't even quite fathom are possible.

The original vegetable of the fae, mushrooms hold secrets like no other vegetable, especially those grown along the forest floor out of sight from humans. Faeries and other elementals simply *love* to reside in, around and alongside them and, as such, mushrooms have a gentle tenderness to them. They're delicious and desire to be treated as such too.

Wisdom holders and gateway secret keepers, mushrooms can truly transport you to your inner child, if you're open to it!

> **Call in Irish Faery Queen Goddess, Aine,**
> **to align with mushroom for the following:**
> Magick + Love + Healing

Goddess Aine and mushrooms offer you healing through allowing the sacred and magickal journey available to your inner child through faerie connection. Use pansies and green pargasite crystals to add to your spiritual practice with mushrooms and Goddess Aine.

Plant allies include:
These are the most aligned flavour boosters and partners that support mushrooms best when cooking and eating:

Herbs: parsley, tarragon, sage, chives, dill
Spices: garlic, chillies, mustards, dried herbs
Vegetables: all root vegetables, dark leafy greens, onions, fennel, cabbages
Fruits: tomatoes, avocado, lemons
Grains/cereals: pastas, rices, couscous, quinoa, flours, pastries, breads, polenta
Beans/legumes: all varieties
Healthy fats: olive oils, avocado oil, macadamia oil, nuts and seeds
Other proteins: soft and firm tofu, tempeh

Market
All varieties must display shiny, bright tops that are free from blemishes, bruising and soft spots. Stems should be intact and show no signs of dampness, as moisture turns mushrooms quickly.

Allow 150–200 g per person, before cooking.

Nurture
All mushrooms must be kept in brown paper bags to prevent 'sweating' while being stored in the fridge, so plastic is a no-no. Mushrooms will keep in your fridge for up to four–five days.

Honour
Mushrooms should never be washed, as they are like little sponges. Wipe over gently with a damp clean tea towel if there happens to be excess soil attached. Simply trim their stems and use as directed in the recipe you are using. Enjoy raw or cooked.

Kitchen helpers
If using large field mushrooms, you can have someone peel away their skins for you or simply snap away the stems.

MUSHROOM RECIPE

Stir-Fry Ginger Mushrooms with Udon

Serves 4
Preparation 15 minutes
Cooking 5 minutes

2 tablespoons macadamia oil
2 green onions, cut into 3 cm lengths
5 cm piece ginger, peeled + cut into thin matchsticks
500 g mixed mushrooms, torn (oyster, Swiss brown, enoki, shitake + button)
2 x 200 g packets shelf-ready udon noodles, gently separated
¼ cup (60 ml) coconut aminos
2 large handfuls baby spinach leaves

1. Heat the oil in a large wok over a high heat. Add the onions and ginger. Cook, stir-frying, for 30 seconds. Add the mushrooms. Cook, stir-frying, for 1–2 minutes or until just tender. Add the noodles and ccoconut aminos, toss together gently until just combined, then remove from heat.
2. Add spinach to the wok and gently toss until just combined and slightly wilting. Season to taste. Serve.

Additions
Add some chopped roasted cashews and a squeeze of lime juice.

Serve alongside
Sliced barbecued proteins, tofu steaks, chicken thigh fillets or beef sirloin.

AUTUMN

Autumn Food and Goddess Initiations

Autumn Is...
Allowing what no longer serves you to fall away easily; celebrations for, and the harvesting of, the soil; gratitude and contentment felt through the fruitful abundance of Mother Earth's love; preparation of foods for the upcoming winter months; coming together and feasting in the season's sweet delights; giving great thanks for all that nurtures our loved ones, our home, the community we gather in and the land we reside on.

Sacred feminine energy for autumn is the Maga: personally empowered with a true knowing of self; intuition gained through life experiences are now turned into great teachings for others.

>**Autumn Magick**
>**Moon cycle is** Last Quarter
>**Element is** Water
>**Direction is** West
>**Time of day is** Morning
>**Tools are** Inner strength and Salt
>**Colours are** Oranges, Reds, Dark Greens and Browns

Kitchen Craft for Autumn
Start to view your kitchen, the heart and soul of your home, as one big altar. The one sacred, temple space where you and

your loved ones can commune together. Try these kitchen (altar) crafts throughout autumn:

Completely dry out thinly sliced rounds of apples in a low-temperature oven and once cooled, string the slices together to make apple garlands that you can hang around your kitchen, especially beside the windows edges or across door frames.

Place gathered fallen autumn leaves together on a tabletop and set a bowl at the centre filled with whole fresh walnuts, still in their shells, for people to gather around and shell as desired. Keep the bowl topped up all season long.

Empowering Words
You can speak these words out loud, write them down in your journal or post them up on your fridge for added personal empowerment through autumn. Try these to start you off, then have a go at writing your own.

> *I am grateful for the abundance in my life.*
> *I let go of what no longer serves me.*
> *My personal wisdom empowers me.*

Autumn Seasoning: Balanced Seasoning
This is the dedicated seasoning blend for autumn. It offers you a balance of sweet and earthy flavours, making it a delicious sprinkle for baked sweet treats after cooking, stirred through your favourite hot mug of tea or used to lightly stew harvest fruits in.

Make this seasoning in one large batch and store in an airtight container in your dry-store cupboard for the duration of the autumn months. Whatever is not used by the end of autumn, simply give thanks to before discarding.

Pound together in a mortar and pestle 2 tablespoons of dried edible crushed rose petals and a large pinch of saffron threads until as fine a powder as you can manage. Transfer the mixture to the storage container you will be using, then add 1 ¼ cups of unrefined coconut sugar. Attach the lid and then using both hands on the jar, shake gently as you make a cross-motion across your heart's space. Do this four times until combined. Store for three days before using for the first time.

Makes approx. 1 ⅓ cups.

Overarching Goddess Dedication: Celtic Goddess Airmed
Goddess Airmed held me tight with Her healing energy throughout autumn and while writing the words to this section of *Priestess Your Plate*. She invoked a need for me to prepare my energy bodies through the use of herbs in all that I cooked in preparation for, and to offer protection to, the upcoming winter months. There's a sense of wanting to gather together, harvest what remains in the herb garden and spend time dedicating to what I can only term best as self-nesting.

> More Autumn Goddesses
> **Incan Goddess ZARAMAMA** – mother of corn
> **Roman Goddess COPIA** – abundant,
>   fertile Mother Earth
> **Greek Goddess DEMETER** – mother of agriculture

Egyptian Goddess MUT – motherly sky deity
Inuit Goddess PUKKEENEGAK – hearth and home
Roman Goddess AUTUMNUS – the epitome of autumn's abundance
Cambodian Goddess PO INO NOGAR – protector of rice
Roman Goddess OPS – nurturing vegetation and humanity

GODDESS INITIATIONS

Call in (ask for) the following Goddesses to be present with you as you journey with their corresponding seasonal food in the upcoming pages:

Figs and **Goddess Aphrodite**
Leeks and **Goddess Freya**
Broccoli and **Goddess Rhiannon**
Green Cabbage and **Goddesses the Zorya**
Apple and **Goddess Pomona**
Pears and **Goddess Oshun**

More in-season foods: pomegranate, quince, kale, pumpkin, brussels sprouts, ginger, Swiss chard, turnip, bok choy.

FOOD SACREDNESS IN AUTUMN
First Month Autumn Rising

In the first month of autumn, we are still feeling the embrace of those summer days but begin to feel the cooler change in the evenings. Time is spent both in equal balance of being outside and inside in all that we do, especially when out selecting foods and eating meals. It's still too warm to turn our ovens on for long periods of time but quick toasting is welcomed for the warming tastes it offers to dishes. We start to enjoy eating meals sitting down with loved ones inside again. We prepare the shelves in our dry-store cupboards, fridge and freezer by cleaning them down in preparation of restocking soon. In this first month of autumn, we will enjoy the end of all fresh herbs and salad leaves that have heavily featured our summer dishes.

Cooking Methods

Toasting
Toasting is to cook or brown food using an element or open fire that can be either directly only from above, on the sides or from below.

Poaching
Poaching is cooking foods in a shallow amount of gently simmering liquid over a low heat.

Recipes
Figs with Saffron and Toasted Pistachio Crumb page 167
Poached Leeks with Mustard Dressing page 170

Figs and Goddess Aphrodite

A perfectly ripe, sweet fig is a ridiculously seductive experience. Figs just love this about themselves, holding such power over your tastebuds that warrant a true love affair when at their peak in the season.

With such a delicate body of flesh, which again represents the beautiful shape of the sacred feminine form, figs really do require a gentle touch and seek for their flavour to be the heroine in any dish. Simply served on their own with a few nuts and a little drizzle of something sweet, like pure maple, is really all they need. Anything else is deemed excessive in their eyes.

Figs have a regal quality to them. They have a very grounded sense of who they are and what immense beauty and pleasure they hold for such a surprisingly small, humble-looking fruit.

> **Call in Greek Goddess of Love, Aphrodite,
> to align with fig for the following:**
> Wisdom + Pleasure + Fertility

Goddess Aphrodite and fig offer you wisdom through beauty. The inner beauty that comes from dedicated love of self and then through the abundance of love that can be shared with others. Use roses and rose quartz crystals to add to your spiritual practice with fig and Goddess Aphrodite.

Plant allies include:
These are the most aligned flavour boosters and partners that support fig best when cooking and eating:

Herbs: bay leaves
Spices: saffron, vanilla, ground ginger, cinnamon
Vegetables: baby fennel, dark leafy greens, salad greens
Fruits: oranges, lemons, limes, berries, grapes
Grains/cereals: flours, pastries, couscous
Healthy fats: nuts and seeds

Market
Choose thin-skinned varieties that show no signs of being overly soft, have tears in their surface or bruising. The fruit's aroma should be sweet and strong and be sure to transport them only ever in a single layer and out of harm's way from other items—not thrown into a bag where they would turn to mush in an instant.

Allow 1–3 fruit per person when serving.

Nurture
Figs should only ever be eaten on the day they are brought home and enjoyed at room temperature too. If you absolutely must, one day stored in the fridge is OK—just make sure that they remain in a single layer and preferably sitting on kitchen paper towel, in case their skins split and their juice starts to ooze out.

Honour
Figs only ever need a light dust-over with a pastry brush, never wash as their skins can easily tear. Prevent bruising by only ever lightly handling, much like a newborn! No knives are required either for preparation; just simply break open gently in your hands to pull apart into halves. Enjoy raw or very lightly warmed through.

Kitchen helpers
It's a beautiful experience to pull apart figs together with someone you love before devouring.

FIG RECIPE

Figs with Saffron and Toasted Pistachio Crumb

Serves 4
Preparation 15 minutes

¾ cup shelled pistachios
1 large pinch saffron threads
1 large pinch cinnamon
8 large ripe figs, torn in half
50 g plain cashew feta, crumbled
⅓ cup (80 ml) pure maple syrup

1. Preheat oven to 200°C/180°C fan-forced. Line a large baking tray with non-stick baking paper. Add pistachios to the prepared tray. Toast for 3–5 minutes or until golden. Cool on tray.
2. Place the saffron and cinnamon in a mortar and pestle, pound until a fine powder forms. Add the pistachios, pound until finely crushed.
3. Arrange the figs, flesh sides facing up, on a serving platter. Top with the feta and the pistachio crumb. Drizzle with the syrup. Serve immediately.

Additions
Add a few small sprigs of baby rocket leaves on top of each fig.

Serve alongside
Thinly sliced, toasted ciabatta that's drizzled with good-quality extra-virgin olive oil.

Leek and Goddess Freya

Leeks have been revered as the most noble of vegetables for thousands of years, with women tending to fenced sacred gardens specifically dedicated to Goddess Freya.

Standing upright with pride and adorned with a sense of armour for protection, leeks have an incredibly tender, soft and sweet centre under it all.

Leeks pride themselves on the comfort they can offer you when cooked slowly and shared with loved ones.

> **Call in Norse Goddess of Love and War, Freya, to align with leek for the following:**
> Beauty + Battle + Divination

On the surface things can look wild and untamed, but at the heart of both Goddess Freya and leek there is such sweet beauty. Use primrose and amber crystals to add to your spiritual practice with leek and Goddess Freya.

Plant allies include:
These are the most aligned flavour boosters and partners that support leek best when cooking and eating:

> **Herbs:** parsley, tarragon, sage, chives, mint, dill
> **Spices:** garlic, mustards, dried oregano, fennel seed
> **Vegetables:** mushrooms, all root vegetables,
>   dark leafy greens, onions
> **Fruits:** lemons
> **Grains/cereals:** rices, pastas, breads, flours, pastries

Beans/legumes: butter, cannellini, lentils, chickpeas
Healthy fats: olive oils
Other proteins: tempeh

Market
Select crisp-looking, brightly coloured medium-sized leeks—too large and their centres are too fibrous.

Allow ¼–½ leek per person when cooking.

Nurture
Leeks will keep in your fridge crisper section wrapped in a clean tea towel for up to one week. Because of the way leeks are grown, with soil piled up around their stems, they can be incredibly dirty on the inside so always require a thorough washing under running tap water as you'll find the soil in between every layer.

Honour
Leeks have such a delicate, sweet flavour and thoroughly enjoy being cooked over low heats and gently, making them such a great addition to soups, stews, in pies and any type of slow-cooked meal. Trim the ends and remove the green tops completely, only ever using the white stalk section of leeks. Peel away one or two layers of the outer leaves before preparing further as directed in your recipe. Enjoy cooked.

Kitchen helpers
Having someone to wash and clean between the layers of leek to remove the soil is a wonderful helping hand to have in the kitchen.

LEEK RECIPE

Poached Leeks with Mustard Dressing

Serves 4
Preparation 20 minutes
Cooking 15 minutes

1 tablespoon wholegrain mustard
1 small clove garlic, crushed
½ cup (125 ml) verjuice
¼ cup (60 ml) extra-virgin olive oil
1 tablespoon dill leaves
4 medium leeks, trimmed, outer leaves removed, well washed + cut in half crossways

1. Place the mustard, garlic, verjuice, oil and dill together in a screw-top jar. Season to taste. Seal tightly, then shake vigorously until well combined and creamy. Set aside.
2. Place leeks in a saucepan and cover with water. Place over a high heat, bring to a boil and then reduce heat to low. Poach, turning leeks over every now and again for 10–12 minutes or until very tender when a skewer is inserted at centre. Carefully drain, then slice each leek in half lengthways.
3. Arrange leeks onto a serving platter. Shake the jar once more to combine the dressing well, then drizzle over. Serve warm.

Additions
Add a good pinch of dried chilli flakes to the dressing. Sprinkle leeks with chopped, roasted walnuts before serving.

Serve alongside
Thick sourdough garlic toasts, or poached chicken breast or fish fillets.

Second Month Autumn Surrender

Most harvest fruits appear at this time in the season and you'll naturally gravitate towards wanting to bake with them more in sweet dishes or add them to your savoury meals. Once again, we desire to gather together around and in the kitchen and at mealtimes. Enjoy having company around to help you select, prepare and cook foods together. As we put more layers of clothes on, we also embrace the foods we eat with a deeper sense of care. We layer flavourings too, and you'll naturally want to start adding more dried herbs and spices to meals.

Cooking Methods

Grilling
A dry, high heat is used from an above element to cook foods quickly.

Pan-frying
Cooking foods over a low, medium or high heat using minimal healthy fats.

Recipes
Grilled Broccoli and Quinoa Salad page 175
Pan-Fried Cabbage and Sage Gnocchi page 179

Broccoli and Goddess Rhiannon

Broccoli has definitely endured a lot over the years and has been disregarded by many, especially young children. However, when cooked lightly, this green goddess can and will be loved by all.

Broccoli holds stature; it stands upright, has a tightly formed floral 'head' and with that green hue really looks regal.

A vegetable that can easily hold its own by simply tossing with a little oil and salt and roasted, broccoli definitely likes to be the heroine in any dish. However, it is more than ready for popular belief to be transcended into a more modern view, so broccoli asks that you consider it as any other super-green vegetable.

> **Call in Welsh Lunar Goddess, Rhiannon,**
> **to align with broccoli for the following:**
> Patience + Movement + Leadership

Goddess Rhiannon and broccoli combine to offer the message of how spiritual development and growth comes through the patience of sacred leadership. Use daffodils and cat's eye crystals to add to your spiritual practice with broccoli and Goddess Rhiannon.

Plant allies include:
These are the most aligned flavour boosters and partners that support broccoli best when cooking and eating:

Herbs: parsley, chives, thyme
Spices: garlic, chillies, ginger
Vegetables: dark leafy greens, onions,
Fruits: lemons, avocado, tomatoes
Grains/cereals: pastas, rices, freekeh, bulgur, couscous, quinoa, pastries
Beans/legumes: all varieties
Healthy fats: olive oils, avocado oil, nuts and seeds
Other proteins: firm tofu, tempeh

Market
Select heads of broccoli with tight firm florets that are brightly coloured and have no yellow patches or show signs of flowering.

Allow ¼ medium head per person when serving.

Nurture
Try to enjoy broccoli soon after purchasing. You can keep heads of broccoli in breathable cloth bags or wrapped in a clean tea towel in the vegetable crisper section of your fridge for up to five days. However, it's best to enjoy within two days.

Honour
Trim the base end of the stem and then snap apart the florets, into equal sized pieces. Don't discard the remaining stem, as it can be sliced or chopped and added to dishes too. Broccoli is best when just cooked until tender, to retain a slight crunch and bright colour, so blanch, grill, stir-fry or quickly roast. Enjoy raw or cooked.

Kitchen helpers
Those young and young at heart will have fun snapping apart the florets for you.

BROCCOLI RECIPE

Grilled Broccoli and Quinoa Salad

Serves 4
Preparation 20 minutes
Cooking 25 minutes

¾ cup quinoa, well rinsed
1 head broccoli, florets separated + stem chopped
1 red onion, cut into thin wedges
¼ cup (60 ml) avocado oil
2 teaspoons smoked paprika
1 bunch flat-leaf parsley, leaves picked + stems finely chopped
1 large lemon, rind finely grated + juiced

1. Cook the quinoa in a saucepan of boiling water for 12–15 minutes or until tender. Drain well, then transfer to a large heatproof serving bowl.
2. Meanwhile, preheat a stovetop grill on high. Place the broccoli, onion, oil and paprika on a baking tray and toss well to coat. Season well. Spread out so that the vegetables are in a single layer on the tray.
3. Cook under the grill for 5–8 minutes, turning once, or until just tender and dark golden. Transfer the mixture to the quinoa in the bowl. Add the parsley and lemon rind and juice. Toss well to combine. Season to taste again. Serve warm.

Additions
Add some roasted pecans, crumbled cashew feta or chopped fresh apple.

Serve alongside
Pan-fried proteins of choice, such as tempeh, fish fillets or chicken tenderloins.

Green Cabbage and Goddesses the Zorya

Cabbage plays a vital role in our energetic system, especially when we desire to literally bring something to life.

Humble as humble can be, cabbage has received a bad rap over the years, and this is purely due to people not understanding how they like most to be cooked. A deliciously pan-fried roasted cabbage or stuffed leaves that have been gently slow-cooked can transcend your tastebuds.

Cabbage wishes to share the message with you that they can be of great energetic support at times of birthing, not necessarily birthing a child (but they said that too), but also bringing to fruition on Mother Earth any creative project, business or idea.

> **Call in Slavic Goddesses of Time, the Zorya, to align with green cabbage for the following:**
> Protection + Fertility + Cycles

Goddess the Zorya and green cabbage offer the message that when we work alongside the trio of mind, body and soul through cycles of time, we can offer ourselves great protection. Use carnation and aquamarine crystals to add to your spiritual practice with green cabbage and Goddess the Zorya.

Plant allies include:
These are the most aligned flavour boosters and partners that support green cabbage best when cooking and eating:

Herbs: parsley, tarragon, sage, chives, dill
Spices: garlic, chillies, mustards, peppers, fennel seeds, coriander seed, carraway
Vegetables: mushrooms, all root vegetables, dark leafy greens, onions, fennel, carrots
Fruits: oranges, lemons, limes
Grains/cereals: pastas, polenta, pastries, flours
Beans/legumes: butter, cannellini, lentils
Healthy fats: olive oils, nuts

Market

Select cabbage that has a tight, compact head of leaves that show no signs of looking dry, withered or discoloured—the outer leaves should be falling away. Pick them up and make sure that they feel heavy for their size and thoroughly inspect to make sure there are no small insects inside either.

Allow ⅛–¼ medium cabbage per person before cooking.

Nurture

Cabbage will keep, wrapped in a clean tea towel, in the vegetable crisper section of your fridge for a week. They love to be cooked until caramelised and nutty in taste or for long periods of cooking with other strong flavours.

Honour

Remove the tougher, outer protective leaves and simply slice, shred or chop as required. You can discard the core as you go or use it also. To form wedges that will stay in shape on cooking, cut thickly with the core still intact. Enjoy raw or cooked.

Kitchen helpers
There is something quite satisfying when you're able to run your fingers between the leaves to separate and pull them apart, with children having the magick touch in being able to do this quickly.

GREEN CABBAGE RECIPE

Pan-Fried Cabbage and Sage Gnocchi

Serves 4
Preparation 15 minutes
Cooking 25 minutes

500 g packet fresh, ready-made potato gnocchi
⅓ cup (80 ml) olive oil
½ medium green cabbage, outer leaves discarded
+ then cut into thick wedges through the core
2 cloves garlic, sliced
Handful sage leaves
1 lemon, rind finely grated + juiced

1. Cook the gnocchi in a large saucepan of gently boiling water for 5–6 minutes or until just tender. Drain well and set aside.
2. Heat the oil in a large, deep frying pan over medium heat. Add the cabbage. Cook, turning occasionally, for 12–15 minutes or until very tender and caramelised. Use tongs to remove to a plate.
3. Add the cooked gnocchi, garlic and sage to the same pan over medium heat. Cook, tossing constantly, for 2–3 minutes or until golden. Remove pan from heat, return cabbage and then add the lemon rind and juice. Toss to combine. Season to taste. Serve.

Additions
Add some thinly sliced green onions and toss through just before serving.

Serve alongside
A crisp Italian-leaf salad mix.

Third Month Autumn Emerging

As we begin to emerge from the energy of autumn there is a strong pull forward into winter's embrace. We can sense it on the horizon and desire to nest ourselves in preparation. This is the most bountiful time for harvest fruits, and we look to ways to prepare and cook this abundance for the winter months through preserving.

Stocking our shelves, fridges and freezers is natural at this time and we pride ourselves on boosting our systems with foods that are great for immunity-building and that will support us best through the colder weather.

We are starting to spend more time indoors and bake sweet goods to share with loved ones or to fill the freezer, again in preparation for the first few weeks of winter where we will want to recoil on our own with a little treat and a hot cup of something alongside it.

Cooking Methods

Sweet baking
Foods cooked in a medium heat, dry environment such as an oven.

Preserving
Preserving is a way of keeping or storing foods for long periods of time without spoiling.

Recipes
Sweet Baked Apples with Pastry Top page 184

Preserved Pears page 187

Other cookery ideas for autumn:
Sweet bakes, cookies, slices and fruit pies or pastries gift you the enjoyment of a sweet treat that isn't too labour-intensive.

Apple and Goddess Pomona

The original fruit of the Goddess, apples are little packages of perfection that resemble the shape of a heart and offer a youthful taste.
Eaten in entirety raw or cooked, apples are a humble, delicious and soul-satisfying fruit that can add crunch to savoury refreshing salads or sweetened further when cooked in old-time favourite baked pies, crumbles, cakes and pastries.
Apples' message is one of majesty and wisdom and a true symbol of love. They really enjoy just being held in your hands and eaten simply as they are.

Call in Roman Goddess of Fruit Orchards, Pomona, to align with apple for the following:
Pleasure + Beauty + Joy

Goddess Pomona and apple share that so much pleasure can come from tending to things of beauty and that with proper care, joy can be cultivated. Use dahlia and sapphire crystals to add to your spiritual practice with apple and Goddess Pomona.

Plant allies include:
These are the most aligned flavour boosters and partners that support apple best when cooking and eating:

> **Herbs:** parsley, chives, chervil
> **Spices:** vanilla, cinnamon, cardamon, nutmeg, mixed spice, ground ginger
> **Vegetables:** salad greens, onions

Fruits: citrus, all orchard fruits
Grains/cereals: couscous, quinoa, flours, pastries
Beans/legumes: butter, cannellini, lentils
Healthy fats: nuts and seeds

Market
Apples are one of those fruits that's always best to purchase either direct from the orchard or at a grower's market where you know that the fruit has literally been picked just hours before. The longer the fruit can be on the tree just before you purchase, the better for absolute best flavour.

Allow 1 whole fruit per person when serving.

Nurture
You can store apples, wrapped up in a tea towel, in your fridge for up to five days to retain their crispness. A quick wash under running tap water is all they require before enjoying.

Honour
Enjoy whole as they are or slice, removing the seeds as you go, and serve. Flavour and fibre are packed just beneath the skin's surface, so the preference is always to leave the skins on when enjoying fresh and depending on the variety used, you may need to peel them before cooking. Enjoy raw or cooked.

Kitchen helpers
Get little hands washing your apples for you in the sink.

APPLE RECIPE

Sweet Baked Apples with Pastry Top

Serves 4
Preparation 20 minutes + 5 minutes resting
Cooking 30 minutes

4 green apples, peeled, cored + cut into thick wedges
2 tablespoons raw sugar, plus 2 tablespoons extra
½ teaspoon ground cinnamon
50 g dairy-free spread, melted
1 x frozen puff pastry sheet, at room temperature
Vanilla nice-cream, to serve

1. Preheat oven to 200°C/180°C fan-forced.
2. Place apples, sugar, cinnamon and all but 2 teaspoons of the melted spread in a 20 cm-wide Pyrex pie dish, tossing well to coat evenly. Bake for 15 minutes or until just starting to collapse and juices are releasing.
3. Carefully cover the apples with the pastry sheet, crimping up the edges. Brush the top with the remaining melted spread, sprinkle with the extra sugar and prick all over with a fork. Bake for a further 12–15 minutes or until the pastry is puffed, cooked and golden. Rest for 5 minutes. Serve warm with vanilla nice-cream.

Additions
Add a few tablespoons of dried fruit in with the apples, such as dried cranberries or sultanas.

Serve alongside
Swap out the nice-cream for your favourite custard, yoghurt or a dollop of cream instead.

Pear and Goddess Oshun

Pears hold and embody the wisdom of the matriarch of your family, full of loving hugs too!

Coming from trees that can fruit for decades, pears wish to share with you that there is an ongoing, lifetime worth of abundance available to you through any of your 'fertile' ideas, wishes or desires—it just comes down to devotion in nurturing.

Pears enjoy being of service to you also, whether held in your hand and eaten raw or cooked in savoury or sweet dishes.

> **Call in Yoruban Goddess of Pleasure, Oshun, to align with pear for the following:**
> Femininity + Fertility + Abundance

Goddess Oshun and pear come together in honour of the sacred feminine form, a true embodiment of femininity, and want to express that simple pleasures can come from taking time to nurture one's self. Use daisy flowers and amber crystals to add to your spiritual practice with pear and Goddess Oshun.

Plant allies include:
These are the most aligned flavour boosters and partners that support pear best when cooking and eating:

> **Herbs:** parsley, chives
> **Spices:** cinnamon, ground ginger, vanilla, saffron, cardamon, mixed spice, nutmeg

Vegetables: salad leaves, celery, baby fennel
Fruits: lemons, berries
Grains/cereals: couscous, quinoa, pastries, flours
Healthy fats: nuts and seeds

Market
Try to purchase pears that still feel firm to the touch and have a slightly softer top near where the stems are. Pears ripen from their core outwards, so purchasing overly soft fruit may turn out to have a too ripened centred for you to enjoy. The skins should be free of tears and blemishes too.

Allow 1 whole fruit per person when serving.

Nurture
Keep pears stored separately and not bundled together in a fruit bowl as they tend to bruise easily and have their skins torn, plus they'll ripen more evenly too. Leave them out on your benchtop, but out of direct sunlight and with good air circulation; they'll keep like this for two–three days.

Honour
Pears can be enjoyed with skins on or off; it's just a personal preference. Halve lengthways to remove their inner core and seeds before using as directed in your recipe. Pears are both delicious served in savoury salads as well as used in sweet dishes. Enjoy raw or cooked.

Kitchen helpers
Once you've halved your pears, ask some little helpers to use a small teaspoon to scoop out the inner core and seeds from the centres.

PEAR RECIPE

Preserved Pears

Serves 4
Preparation 30 minutes
Cooking 20 minutes

1 kg white sugar
½ cup (125 ml) golden syrup
½ cup (125 ml) apple cider vinegar
1 cup (250 ml) clear apple juice
4 vanilla pods, split lengthways + seeds scraped
4 cinnamon sticks, broken in half
8 large firm green pears, peeled, quartered + cores removed

1. Place sugar, syrup, vinegar, juice, vanilla pods and seeds and cinnamon together in a large non-reactive saucepan over a medium heat. Cook, stirring constantly, until the sugar has completely dissolved. Simmer for 5 minutes. Reduce heat slightly to a gentle simmer.
2. Carefully add pears to the syrup. Gently simmer for 15 minutes or until just tender—you don't want them falling apart.
3. Using tongs, place the pear pieces into hot sterilised jars, then pour over the hot syrup to cover the fruit completely. Seal tightly and stand until room temperature. Store for at least 1 month before using. Once opened, refrigerate any leftovers. Use within 1 year.

To sterilise jars: simply wash jars in hot soapy water to clean, then rinse in hot water. Place on the open shelves of a low-temperature oven and heat for 30–40 minutes or until completely dry and heated. You may like to use six small jars, two medium-sized ones or one large jar for storing the preserved pears in.

Additions
Add whole spices such as cardamom pods, clove or star anise to the syrup mixture before simmering.

Serve alongside
Warming breakfast oats, turn into a simple dessert with a coconut custard or eat simply as they are with an almond shortbread cookie alongside a hot cuppa.

WINTER

Winter Food and Goddess Initiations

Winter Is...
The death of all that needs to go; a deep surrendering into the self; a time of soul connections to ancestors passed and for honouring your consciousness through journaling; grounded connection through enjoying shared feasts with loved ones that honour your food culture and reignite fond childhood memories; time to be at ease with stillness, journey with rest and use meditation as a sacred tool.

Sacred feminine energy for winter is the Crone: wisdom gained through ageing; a compassionate loving heart; the guiding matriarch of a family unit and the one to look to for a knowledgeable ear.

>   **Winter Magick**
>   **Moon cycle is** New Moon
>   **Element is** Earth
>   **Direction is** South in Southern Hemisphere
>   / North in Northern Hemisphere
>   **Time of day is** Midnight
>   **Tools are** Cleansing and Water
>   **Colours are** Blacks, Dark Purples,
>   Midnight Blue and Silver

Kitchen Craft for Winter
Start to view your kitchen, the heart and soul of your home, as one big altar. The one sacred, temple space where you and

your loved ones can commune together. Try these kitchen (altar) crafts throughout winter:

Set up an ancestral shrine in your kitchen space, placing a piece of fabric underneath (blacks, dark purples, midnight blue or silver) and add photographs of ancestors passed with small tea light candles around. Add fallen twigs, seedpods or other fallen gifts from trees from your garden. Light the candles just before eating each night-time meal and allow them to burn out completely before replacing with new candles for the next evening.

Combine together, in a small (110 ml) spritzer bottle filled with purified water, 7 drops each of nutmeg, clove and bergamot and use as an air mist at times when the energy in your kitchen space may feel heavy.

Empowering Words
You can speak these words out loud, write them down in your journal or post them up on your fridge for added personal empowerment through wintertime. Try these to start you off, then have a go at writing your own.

> *I allow my whole self to surrender.*
> *I receive the shadow with love and compassion.*
> *I slow down and rest in stillness.*

Winter Seasoning: Deep Surrender Salt
This is the dedicated seasoning blend for winter, an earthy blend that will warm you from within. It can be used to season vegetables and proteins of choice before or after slow

cooking for hours either in the oven, in a slow-cooker or on the stovetop.

Make this salt in one large batch and store in an airtight container in your dry-store cupboard for the duration of the winter months. Whatever is not used by the end of winter, simply give thanks to before discarding.

Pound together in a mortar and pestle 2 tablespoons of dried mixed mushrooms (preferably a forest blend) and 1 teaspoon of dried chilli flakes until as fine a powder as you can manage. Transfer the mixture to the storage container you will be using, then add ¾ cup of sea salt flakes. Attach the lid, then using both hands on the jar, shake gently and in a clockwise circular motion for 3 full rounds until combined. Store for 3 days before using for the first time.

Makes approximately ⅔ cup.

Overarching Goddess Dedication: Celtic Goddess Cerridwen
Goddess Cerridwen came to me on my birthday, which just so happens to be Her celebration day in July too, and with full force. As quickly as She arrived, She had left. This is Her directness. I also learned quite quickly how gruff or lack of patience is shown if you double-ask for something or check anything shared for clarity. She will provide information to you once and you better be ready, listening intently to receive it. Quite the task when you're unaware of when it is She may just turn up.

Cerridwen is a crone Goddess that works on Her own timeline, and not particularly easy to call-in as you wish.

Thank Goddess that the deep surrender of winter allows for heightened awareness, as I really believe if Her energy was dedicated to the summer months instead, you'd easily miss Her through all of the noise that those months bring. With Her sacred cauldron, She truly guided the magick behind the words through these pages. I was able to expand time and my energy, especially on those really cold days throughout the season. She awoke within me my own sacred medicine with herbs and spices. I found myself wanting to blend tinctures, use a mortar and pestle more and spent hours at the stovetop and oven caring for hours-long slow-cooked meals. Slowly stirring every now and again.

> More Winter Goddesses
> **Inuit Goddess SEDNA** – the ocean underworld
> **Slavic Goddess MARZANNA** – ruler of dark winter
> **Irish Goddess BADB** – shape-shifting warrior
> **German Goddess MOTHER HOLLE**
>   – winter's wise queen
> **Japanese Goddess INARI** – protects
>   and guides spirits
> **Russian Goddess BABA YAGA** – wild witch
> **Nordic Goddess ELLE** – old age
> **Roman Goddess LARA** – Mother of the dead

GODDESS INITIATIONS

Call in (ask for) the following Goddesses to be present with you as you journey with their corresponding seasonal food in the upcoming pages:

Celeriac and **Goddess Isis**
Sweet Potato **and Goddess Hecate**
Lemon and **Goddess Frigg**
Beetroot and **Goddess Kali Ma**
Rhubarb and **Goddess Hel**
Dates and **The Morrigan**

More in-season foods: kiwi fruit, mandarin, oranges, strawberry, fennel, Jerusalem artichoke, parsnips, silverbeet, swede, turnip.

FOOD SACREDNESS IN WINTER

First Month Winter Rising

We really start to come home to ourselves in this first turn of winter. You'll want to bulk-purchase foods, make big-batch meals and will have your dry food store filled with a mixture of dried herbs and spices, especially those warming ones like cumin, cinnamon and chillies. Once again, you'll minimise your time outside surrounded by others and will take great comfort in menu planning ahead and feeling well-prepared for evening mealtimes as the days start to stay darker for longer. Soups and roasts start to appear now as they offer the bonus of providing enough to eat at dinnertime and then also gift the opportunity for leftovers the next day. There's a sense of wanting to come together at mealtimes.

Cooking Methods

Soups
Food cooked in liquid that gently bubbles away over a low-medium heat source and can be served as is or blended until smooth.

Roasting
Cooking suitable foods through a dry heat in a closed environment (oven or hooded barbecue) and at a higher temperature than usual for a shorter cooking time.

Recipes
Celeriac Soup with Dukkah Flatbreads page 198
Roasted Sweet Potatoes with Harissa Barley page 202

Celeriac and Goddess Isis

A multifaceted vegetable, celeriac is winter personified.

Celeriac shares that not all is what it seems with this humble vegie. Their large shapes, knobbly exterior and quick browning flesh after peeling would indicate fragility, but no—celeriac can shape-shift themselves on demand. Their taste is part potato, part turnip, part celery and they have the ability to be mashed, served raw, roasted, fried, sautéed and pureed too without compromising their texture or flavour in any way

They wish to be seen as the edible embodiment of the wise, old witch, crone aspect of the sacred feminine and the noble sacred masculine.

> **Call in Egyptian Goddess of Magick, Isis, to align with celeriac for the following:**
> Rebirth + Shape-shift + Creatrix

Goddess Isis and celeriac come with a strong presence of knowing their place on the earthly plane—who they are and what they are able to support you with. Offering myriad ways that you can connect with them both, and at a very deep level—true soul nourishment! Use blue water lily and lapis lazuli crystals to add to your spiritual practice with celeriac and Goddess Isis.

Plant allies include:
These are the most aligned flavour boosters and partners that support celeriac best when cooking and eating:

Herbs: parsley, tarragon, sage, chives, chervil, basil, dill
Spices: garlic, mustards, fennel seeds, carraway,
Vegetables: all root vegetables, cabbages, dark leafy greens, onions, fennel, celery
Fruits: lemons, apples
Grains/cereals: rices, millet, bulgur, couscous, quinoa
Beans/legumes: butter, cannellini, lentils
Healthy fats: olive oils, avocado oil, nuts
Other proteins: tempeh

Market
Choose celeriac that are a decent size but not enormous, as these ones tend to have hollow sections inside where you may find small insects gathering. They should feel heavy for their size, like a baseball weight, and still have visibly green tops. Even if the green leaves have been removed, the remaining stems should still appear green and crisp. The surface shouldn't look dull or dried out either.

Allow approximately 200 g per person, before cooking.

Nurture
Celeriac can be stored in the vegetable crisper section of your fridge for up to one week and don't require covering either; their thick outer layer helps to protect them well.

Honour
You'll need to use a large knife to trim the base and tops, stand them upright and then remove the outer skin layer, making sure to discard all the knobbly bits and any excess soil caught in the thick wrinkles too. Once peeled and

chopped, if you are not immediately cooking with celeriac you'll need to place in acidulated water (i.e., a bowl of water with plenty of lemon slices) to prevent the flesh from browning. Enjoy raw or cooked.

Kitchen helpers
Have someone on hand to help you to immerse peeled pieces of celeriac into bowls of lemon water to stop the vegetable from browning.

CELERIAC RECIPE

Celeriac Soup with Dukkah Flatbreads

Serves 4
Preparation 20 minutes
Cooking 35 minutes

2 tablespoons olive oil, plus 2 tablespoons extra
4 flatbreads
2 tablespoons dukkah
2 onions, chopped
2 cloves garlic, chopped
500 g peeled celeriac, chopped
6 cups (1.5 litres) vegetable stock

1. Preheat oven to 180°C/160°C fan-forced. Brush the flatbreads evenly with the oil, then sprinkle with the dukkah. Bake directly on open oven shelves for 8–10 minutes or until light golden and crisp. Set aside.
2. Meanwhile, heat the extra oil in a large saucepan over medium heat. Add onion, garlic and celeriac. Cook, stirring occasionally, for 10 minutes or until starting to soften and light golden. Add stock, stir until mixture comes to a simmer. Reduce heat slightly and gently simmer, partially covered and stirring occasionally, for 20–25 minutes or until the celeriac is very tender and falling apart.
3. Remove the pan from heat. Use a handheld stick mixer to blend the soup until smooth. Season to taste. Serve with the dukkah flatbreads.

Additions
Add carrot and swede along with the celeriac when cooking the soup.

Serve alongside
Add some wilted greens to your bowl before pouring over the soup. Try kale or silverbeet.

Sweet Potato and Goddess Hecate

Sweet potatoes are one of those vegetables that wish for you to explore and experiment with them. Being so versatile and openly adventurous, the sweet potatoes message is to get excited about all the possibilities—sweet pies and savoury dishes, plus fritters, scones, gnocchi, stuffed and blended into soups—they're waiting and ready!

Like many other root vegetables, sweet potatoes offer you and your energetic body amazing grounding capabilities throughout wintertime. The difference with sweet potatoes is that, not only will they ground your energy, at the same time they're able to lift your energy too because of their natural sweetness boost.

> **Call in Greek Goddess of Crossroads, Hecate, to align with sweet potato for the following:**
> Empowerment + Magic + Transformation

Goddess Hecate and sweet potato wish to share that great transformation will occur when we journey through those turning points in life. Trust the magick in the unfolding. Use dandelion and black tourmaline crystals to add to your spiritual practice with sweet potato and Goddess Hecate.

Plant allies include:
These are the most aligned flavour boosters and partners that support sweet potato best when cooking and eating:

> **Herbs:** parsley, sage, chives, oregano, basil, rosemary

Spices: garlic, chillies, mustards, ginger, cinnamon, nutmeg, peppers
Vegetables: mushrooms, dark leafy greens, onions
Fruits: oranges, lemons, limes, tomatoes, avocado
Grains/cereals: rices, pearl barley, couscous, quinoa
Beans/legumes: butter, cannellini, lentils, red kidney, chickpeas
Healthy fats: olive oils, avocado oil, nuts and seeds
Other proteins: firm tofu, tempeh

Market
Available in a variety of coloured skins and flesh, choose sweet potatoes that are free from any dark spots. Their skins should be smooth and look bright.

Allow 2 small or 1 medium sweet potato per person when serving.

Nurture
Store your sweet potatoes in a cool, dark place that is well ventilated, and you'll have a good week before needing to use them.

Honour
Simply wash the skins before using, or peel if desired. Sweet potatoes can be boiled, steamed, roasted, slow-cooked and mashed, just to name a few ways. They enjoy being served simply or added in with other great, deep flavours as well; a truly openly versatile vegetable they are! Enjoy cooked.

Kitchen helpers
Having another person help to peel sweet potatoes for you is always a welcome invite.

SWEET POTATO RECIPE

Roasted Sweet Potatoes with Harissa Barley

Serves 4
Preparation 15 minutes
Cooking 55 minutes

4 x 250 g orange sweet potatoes
⅔ cup pearl barley
2 tablespoons olive oil
2 teaspoons harissa paste
1 red onion, finely chopped
¼ cup finely chopped herbs (rosemary, oregano + flat-leaf parsley)
1 small lemon, rind finely grated + juiced

1. Preheat oven to 180°C/160°C fan-forced. Place the sweet potatoes directly on the oven racks. Roast for 45–50 minutes or until tender when a skewer easily inserts at the centres. Transfer to a serving platter, then split in half lengthways.
2. Meanwhile, cook the barley in a large saucepan of boiling water over a high heat for 35–40 minutes or until just tender. Drain well. Set aside.
3. Heat the oil in the same saucepan over a medium heat. Add the onion and paste. Cook, stirring occasionally for 5 minutes or until very soft and starting to colour. Return the barley, add the herbs and lemon rind and juice. Season to taste. Stir to combine well. Spoon into centres of the sweet potatoes. Serve.

Additions
Add some baby spinach leaves to the barley mixture, stirring until wilted.

Serve alongside
Your favourite roasted protein of choice, such as tempeh, beef fillet or salmon steak.

Second Month Winter Surrender

Deep surrendering into self at home is a must at this time of winter. Here, we go within and enjoy richly flavoured, slow-roasted meals and decadent sweets like puddings, bakes and pies that really nourish our souls and transport us back to fond memories of childhood. This is the month where you don't want to be outside at all and so welcome home-delivery services for your food needs at this time. We really slow down in the kitchen—no quick movements or methods here, and we enjoy taking our time in preparing. Honour the food you have, and the longer time frames taken to cook them, just as you honour yourself and go within. Solo food preparation and cooking is most suited now, as too many people around in your kitchen space will feel overwhelming to your energy bodies. This is time for self-indulgence in all areas. A wanting to sit down and feast with loved ones is essential in this month and foods placed at the centre of the table allows for many hands to help themselves.

Cooking Methods

Puddings
A baked, boiled or steamed richly sweet dish that comes after a main meal.

Slow-Roasting
Although not technically roasting, as temperatures for cooking are low, a dry heat source is used (usually in an oven) for long periods of time.

Recipes
Little Lemon Puddings page 208

Slow-Roasted Beetroot Curry page 212

Lemon and Goddess Frigga

Sunshine yellow lemons are always at their peak of abundance throughout winter, even though they're available year-round.

Lemons will journey with you however you wish, in wanting to be of true service to you. The Priestess of the fruit world, lemons love to be used equally across savoury and sweet dishes and in wintertime ask that you think of them being used particularly in food from your past. Traditional family recipes that you remember fondly, whether that be a lemon meringue pie, tart lemon slice or that Chinese take-out of fried lemon chicken you shared weekly with loved ones.

Lemons are humble and don't desire to be on display in all their grandness. They want to share again that they're here to be of greatest service to you through wintertime while you surrender deeply.

> **Call in Norse Goddess of Marriage, Frigga, to align with lemon for the following:**
> Domesticity + Marriage + Multifaceted

Goddess Frigga and lemon are so aligned, 'marrying' each other well, in their capacity to each honour and hold space for every facet and aspect of who they are. Goddess Frigga being of service to children, women and matrons and lemons being of service from their rinds to their flesh in both sweets and savories, juiced, raw or cooked.

Use mistletoe and aventurine crystals to add to your spiritual practice with lemon and Goddess Frigga.

Plant allies include:
These are the most aligned flavour boosters and partners that support lemon best when cooking and eating:

>**Herbs:** all fresh herbs
>**Spices:** garlic, chillies, mustards, ginger, cardamom, peppers, cumin, paprika, all dried herbs
>**Vegetables:** broccoli, zucchini, onions, root vegetables, celery, carrots, cabbages
>**Fruits:** citrus, berries, stone fruit, tropical fruits, avocado
>**Grains/cereals:** rices, pastas, millet, bulgur, couscous, quinoa, pastries, flours
>**Beans/legumes:** all varieties
>**Healthy fats:** olive oils, avocado oil, macadamia oil, nuts and seeds
>**Other proteins:** soft and firm tofu, tempeh

Market
Choose fruit that are literally bursting with bright yellow skins and feel heavy in juice weight for their size.

Allow ½–1 whole fruit per person when serving, depending on use.

Nurture
Lemons will store beautifully in your fruit bowl out on your kitchen benchtop through wintertime for a couple of weeks; they are gorgeous to look at and will give you a burst

of energy just looking at them. Pick one up every now and again and give a squeeze while deeply breathing in their citrusy oil aroma for an instant clarifying moment or when seeking focus.

Honour
You can zest or finely grate lemons rinds, being sure to leave the white bitter pith behind. Lemons can be prepared in halves, sliced or wedges and even have all skin and white pith removed before segmenting too. Enjoy raw, juiced or in cooked dishes.

Kitchen helpers
Lemons are more often than not sold with a thin wax coating on them, so have some helping hands wash them in warm water for you and dry the skins with a clean tea towel, especially before zesting or grating the rinds for use.

LEMON RECIPE

Little Lemon Puddings

Serves 4
Preparation 20 minutes
Cooking 20 minutes

125 g dairy-free spread
1 cup caster sugar
⅔ cup apple puree
¾ cup self-raising flour
½ cup desiccated coconut
1 large lemon, rind finely grated + juiced
Icing sugar, to dust

1. Preheat oven to 180°C/160°C fan-forced. Grease 4 x ½ cup capacity ramekins.
2. Melt the spread in a saucepan over a low heat. Remove the pan from the heat. Add sugar and stir until combined. Transfer mixture to a bowl. Add puree, flour, coconut, lemon rind and juice. Stir until well combined.
3. Divide mixture evenly among the prepared ramekins. Bake for 15–18 minutes or until cooked when a skewer inserted at centres comes out clean. Rest for 5 minutes, then dust tops with icing sugar. Serve warm.

Additions
Add 1 teaspoon of ground cardamom to the lemon mixture before baking.

Serve alongside
Dollop with a scoop of your favourite nice-cream.

Beetroot and Goddess Kali Ma

Seductive, earthy and deeply nourishing, beetroot are the ultimate, great symbols of the heart.

Beetroot desire to share their message of whole-self wellbeing through relaxation, and to use them in your meals as the comforting guide to aid this for you.

A meal using beetroot will also invoke deep love and compassion, regardless of whether you wish to enjoy this for yourself as you deepen into the winter months or whether you are gathering together with those closest to you to enjoy a shared meal.

> **Call in Hindu Fierce Mother Goddess of Transformation, Kali Ma, to align with beetroot for the following:**
> Destruction + Creation + Liberation

Goddess Kali Ma and beetroot share that by removing all preconceived notions of what something should be—destroying it in entirety—and starting right back at the point of creation, with love and compassion, will ultimately provide more liberation. Use hibiscus and snowflake obsidian crystals to add to your spiritual practice with beetroot and Goddess Kali Ma.

Plant allies include:
These are the most aligned flavour boosters and partners that support beetroot best when cooking and eating:

Herbs: parsley, tarragon, chives, chervil, basil, mint, coriander, dill
Spices: garlic, chillies, mustards, ginger, dried spices
Vegetables: potatoes, dark leafy greens, onions, all root vegetables, brassicas, celery
Fruits: oranges, lemons, apples, tomatoes
Grains/cereals: rices, millet, bulgur, couscous, quinoa, polenta, pearl barley
Beans/legumes: butter, cannellini, lentils
Healthy fats: olive oils, avocado oil, nuts and seeds
Other proteins: tempeh

Market
Beetroot should look bright, have rich red colour and have smooth skins, and only purchase bunches that have their stalks and leaves still intact so that you can use these edible gems also in your dishes. The stalks and leaves may seem droopy but this is OK—it happens not long after harvest.

Allow 1 medium size or 3–4 baby beetroot per person when serving.

Nurture
Trim the leaves, but not too close to the top of the beetroot (leave a good 4 cm), and store in the vegetable crisper section of your fridge, wrapped in a clean tea towel for up to one week. Keep the stalks and leaves in a separate container lined with kitchen paper towel.

Honour
You can simply scrub the skins of beetroot, no need to peel. Beetroots do require time to cook, so if cutting be sure that

all pieces are of the same size for even tenderness. Enjoy raw or cooked.

Kitchen helpers
When roasting whole beetroot until tender, and after they have cooled, have someone help easily slip off the skins to discard before using further.

BEETROOT RECIPE

Slow-Roasted Beetroot Curry

Serves 4
Preparation 20 minutes + 5 minutes standing
Cooking 1 hour 5 minutes

¼ cup rogan josh curry paste
1 onion, chopped
3 cm piece ginger, peeled + finely chopped
1 x 400 g can chopped tomatoes
2 bunches baby beetroot, washed well, then halved + stems chopped and leaves kept
1 x 400 g can chickpeas, drained, well rinsed + drained again
½ cup coriander leaves

1. Preheat oven to 160°C/140°C fan-forced.
2. Place a flameproof, heavy-based roasting pan over a medium heat. Add the paste, onion and ginger. Cook, stirring, for 3 minutes or until starting to soften. Add tomatoes, beetroot and 1 cup (250 ml) water. Stir until the mixture comes to a simmer, then immediately cover and transfer to the oven. Slow-roast for 1 hour or until beetroot are tender when a skewer is inserted at centre.
3. Remove pan from the oven, stir through chickpeas, reserved beetroot stems and leaves. Stand covered for 5 minutes. Serve sprinkled with coriander.

Additions
Stir through baby spinach leaves and chopped roasted almonds before serving.

Serve alongside
Toasted naan bread, cooked basmati rice and plain coconut yoghurt.

Third Month Winter Emerging

It's still exceptionally cold outside and dark but there is a pull forward into the brightness that spring offers. The horizon feels near! Rich-tasting sweets and desserts still feature heavily here but we start to pull away from intensive preparation of meals and look towards using a slow-cooker appliance more rather than having the oven on for hours on end. You may desire to emerge from home and begin shopping around others again. Your pantry, fridge and freezer may begin to feel almost bare and that a good ol' top-up is required to replenish them all. Enjoying meals around a table with loved ones is still present but the sense of wanting to feast is no longer there.

Cooking Methods

Stews
A dish where foods are cooked together in one pot with small amounts of liquid over a low-medium heat while covered. Can be short or long cooking times as well as for sweet or savoury foods.

Slow-Cooker Cooking
An electric pot that is used for cooking foods with small amounts of liquid, covered and using a low temperature for long periods of time.

Recipes
Stewed Rhubarb Crumble page 218
Slow-Cooker Sticky Date Choc Cake page 221

Other cookery ideas for winter:
Deep-frying
Deep-fried doughnuts, vegetable chips or tempura fruits are deliciously warming and decadent ways to enjoy sweets in winter.

Mashing
Mashing together steamed or boiled root vegetables and then serving alongside your favourite protein of choice is one of the easiest and most satisfying meals to consume in winter. It's a great way to use up odd bits and pieces of vegetables that you have in your fridge too.

Rhubarb and Goddess Hel

Rhubarb literally forces its way up and out of the ground with such strength that their stalks are perfectly upright, standing proud in their wisdom.

A fierce vegetable, although widely known as a fruit, in the sense that She is only edible once cooked and needs either added sweetness for desserts or deep spice flavours for savoury dishes and chutneys to be able to make Her palatable.

The embodiment of the dark crone, rhubarb's fibrous flesh only becomes less bitter once carefully cooked—low and slow. Rhubarb makes you handle Her with care, as her leaves are poisonous and should never be eaten.

> **Call in Norse Goddess and Queen**
> **of the Underworld, Hel,**
> **to align with rhubarb for the following:**
> Strong + Powerful + Fierce

Goddess Hel and rhubarb come together with their message of strength and that a good balance of fierceness can be a powerful force. Use ivy and onyx crystals to add to your spiritual practice with rhubarb and Goddess Hel.

Plant allies include:
These are the most aligned flavour boosters and partners that support rhubarb best when cooking and eating:

> **Herbs:** parsley, tarragon, sage, chives, chervil, basil,

Spices: vanilla, cinnamon, ground ginger, cardamom
Vegetables: tomato, mushrooms, potatoes, dark leafy greens, onions
Fruits: citrus, apples, berries, stone fruit
Grains/cereals: pastry, couscous, quinoa
Beans/legumes: butter, cannellini, lentils
Healthy fats: nuts

Market
Winter rhubarb has the deepest red colour of all the rhubarb grown throughout the year. Select stalks that have vibrant colour and are very firm, as rhubarb loses its freshness quickly; lifeless stalks are a very good indicator of age after picking.

Allow ¼ bunch per person, before cooking.

Nurture
Always best used within two days of selecting and bringing home to your kitchen. They can be trimmed and cleaned, then wrapped in a clean tea towel and kept in your fridge for up to one week.

Honour
Remove and discard the top poisonous leaves and trim away the brown base ends too. Chop or cut into sections as directed. Rhubarb breaks down quickly and easily, so it doesn't require too much liquid when cooking as it can turn into a rough puree in an instant. Delicious in savoury foods as well as sweet, rhubarb particularly loves being baked into desserts and other sweet treats. Enjoy cooked.

Kitchen helpers
If your rhubarb happens to be quite stringy, let some little hands pull them away.

RHUBARB RECIPE

Stewed Rhubarb Crumble

Serves 6–8
Preparation 25 minutes
Cooking 35 minutes

2 bunches rhubarb, trimmed + cut into 2 cm pieces
¼ cup caster sugar
2 teaspoons ground ginger
100 g untoasted muesli
¾ cup plain flour
½ cup brown sugar
100 g dairy-free spread

1. Preheat oven to 180°C/160°C fan-forced. Grease a 6-cup capacity baking dish.
2. Place rhubarb, caster sugar, ginger and ½ cup (125 ml) water in a large, deep frying pan over medium heat. Cook, stirring gently, for 1 minute until the sugar dissolves. Reduce heat to low and cook, covered and gently shaking pan occasionally for 5 minutes or until very tender. Transfer mixture to prepared baking dish.
3. Combine muesli, flour, brown sugar and spread in a bowl. Using your fingers, rub the mixture together until it resembles large crumbs. Sprinkle over rhubarb in the dish. Bake for 25–30 minutes or until the top is golden. Stand for 5 minutes. Serve warm.

Additions
Hull and halve a punnet of strawberries and scatter over the stewed rhubarb in the baking dish before adding the crumble mixture and baking.

Serve alongside
A dish of thickly whipped coconut cream.

Dates and The Morrigan

Dates are Mother Earth's natural sweet-tasting, chewy caramels!

A delicacy and true fruit of the High Priestess, dates wish to be honoured for their addictive intensity and instant burst of energy they can offer you, especially at wintertime when you can feel sluggish and lack energy.

Dates have been cherished for thousands of years for the small golden jewels that they are and are still sacred place holders in cultures today.

> **Call in Irish Witch Queen Goddess, Morrigan, to align with dates for the following:**
> Magick + Prophecy + Sovereignty

Goddess Morrigan and dates combine together through the power of abundance and signify that sovereignty can be gained through small amounts of shape-shifting. Use willow and garnet crystals to add to your spiritual practice with dates and Goddess Morrigan.

Plant allies include:
These are the most aligned flavour boosters and partners that support dates best when cooking and eating:

> **Herbs:** parsley, chives, coriander, mint
> **Spices:** ground ginger, saffron, cardamon
> **Vegetables:** all root vegetables, dark
>   leafy greens, onions

Fruits: oranges, lemons, limes, all dried fruits
Grains/cereals: rices, couscous, quinoa, flours, pastries
Healthy fats: nuts and seeds

Market
Choose plump fruit, with their pips still in place, which have a shiny skin and show no signs of damage from over-handling. The fruit also shouldn't be tightly compressed into the packaging they've been transported in.

Allow 3–4 whole fresh dates per person when serving.

Nurture
With their high sugar content, dates are best stored in the fridge in a container and will last for weeks and remain fairly plump. If left at room temperature, they will dry out and become tough.

Honour
Dates' beauty is that they require very little prep work, simply break open and discard their pips before using as directed in your recipes. Enjoy raw or cooked.

Kitchen helpers
Have someone help remove the pips for you; just make sure to add a few more in as they're pretty irresistible to not munch on in the process!

DATE RECIPE

Slow-Cooker Sticky Date Choc Cake

Serves 4
Preparation 15 minutes + 5 minutes standing
Cooking 1 hour 35 minutes

200 g fresh dates, seeds removed, chopped
1 ¼ cups self-raising flour
¼ cup cocoa powder, sifted
½ cup brown sugar, plus 1 cup extra
⅔ cup (160 ml) milk of choice
½ cup apple puree
50 g melted dairy-free spread, plus 40 g extra
2 cups (500 ml) boiling water

1. Place the dates, flour, cocoa and sugar together in a bowl, stir until well combined. Add the milk, puree and melted spread. Stir until well combined.
2. Grease the base and side of a slow-cooker bowl with half of the extra spread. Spoon in date mixture, level surface. Evenly sprinkle the top with the extra sugar and dot all over with the remaining spread. Carefully pour over the boiling water.
3. Cover and set on High. Slow-cook for 1 hour and 35 minutes or until cooked when a skewer inserted at centre of cake comes out clean. Remove the bowl from the machine. Stand covered for 5 minutes. Serve warm.

Additions
Add a little ground cinnamon and nutmeg to the date mixture before slow-cooking.

Serve alongside
Dollop with your favourite choice of yoghurt, cream or nice-cream.

CLOSING CEREMONY

A Closing Vow

I, Priestess Tracey Mary Isobel Meharg Pattison, close these sacred pages.

My closing vow to you is my devotion in continuing this Divine work, however our great Mother Earth requires through Her seasons.

May you move forward on your own journey now, in complete food sovereignty.

Priestess Your Plate, delicious one.

And so it is.

Priestess Your Plate Path Forward

Be sure to head to www.traceypattison.com/pyp-book to receive your Sacred Food Journey Meditation and the Heart-mapping Your Journey Guide, plus some additional bonuses that will support your journey further.

I want to take this time to bow to you with such deep gratitude in your service to this shift of consciousness for all women-identifying. Whether you have been actively conscious through this shift or whether this is the first time you've read of it—you have taken part and made this possible. Just by accepting your soul's call to reside on Mother Earth at this time in the cosmos, and placing your hands on this book to read Her pages—you answered that call and you have done the work needed for right here, right now at this very moment.

May you live a life so deliciously empowered by the food you choose to nourish yourself with so that you can lead (Priestess) out in the world ALL that your heart desires, be that as a parent, teacher, healer, space holder, coach, entrepreneur, business owner, light-worker or community member.

May you find your own heart's compass towards how you *Priestess Your Plate* through food sovereignty, sacredness and the gained intuition of your inner cycles of self within the seasons of our Great Mother Earth.

May you remember, surrender to and be guided by the foundation of what makes you, YOU. Your ancestry, where you reside, your stories and your best life envisioned.

> *You are Divine.*
> *I hold you.*
> *I see you.*
> *I am here for you.*
> *And*
> *I thank you.*

From my soul to your soul, from my kitchen to yours, and until our spirits commune again.

With Priestess Love, delicious one.

Tracey x

Recipe Notes

Please note that the recipes are written using Australian Standard weights and measures. Use cups and measuring spoons for dry and solid ingredients and jugs for measuring any liquids. Tablespoon measures: I have used 20 ml (4 teaspoon) tablespoon measures. If you're using 15 ml (3 teaspoon) tablespoon, add an extra teaspoon of the ingredient for each tablespoon specified.

Oven temperatures

Celsius (electric)	Celsius (fan-forced)	Fahrenheit	Gas	
120º	100º	250º	1	very slow
150º	130º	300º	2	slow
160º	140º	325º	3	moderately slow
180º	160º	350º	4	moderate
190º	170º	375º	5	moderately hot
200º	180º	400º	6	hot
230º	210º	450º	7	very hot
250º	230º	500º	9	very hot

Always preheat your oven for at least 15 minutes before using and check the manufacturer's instructions for any further adjustments. It's great practice to check your food 10 minutes before the total cooking time mentioned in the recipe also as ovens can run hot, especially when set on fan-forced.

Priestess Gratitude

To my husband and our two children: your unconditional love and acceptance is my constant drive and inspiration to be all that I can be, for you.

To my publisher, Natasha Gilmour, who first witnessed me explaining what these pages of *Priestess Your Plate* could be, I feel so grateful for the absolute excitement and deep connection you felt for Her from that first experience—I simply cannot express with these simple words the love I have for you and your belief in me and Her. To be held, witnessed and honoured so completely by you and the kind press team has been a pivotal moment in my life. A publishing experience I never thought possible.

To all of the women I've journeyed with on my spiritual path from Soulpreneurs to Priestess Temple School, Ellie Swift's marketing mastermind and inner circle and Sammie Fleming's sacred biz spaces—you've ALL had an impact on me and witnessed the seeds of this being birthed. All which has led to me being able to share my voice through these pages. This is something I will be forever eternally grateful for. We are the Priestesses, Witches and Goddesses of all time.

And to the women and men of my ancestry—those passed and those yet to come forward—thank you, thank you, for your love and all that you endured and celebrated to make it possible for me to be in this moment right now.

Bibliography

Alexander, Stephanie. *The Cooks Companion*. Penguin Lantern 2004.

Auset, Brandi. *The Goddess Guide: Exploring the Attributes and Correspondences of the Divine Feminine*. Llewellyn Publications 2009.

Danu, Forest. *The Magical Year, Seasonal Celebrations to Honour Nature's Ever-turning Wheel*. Watkins Media Limited, First published 2016.

Silja. *The Green Wiccan Herbal, 52 Magical Herbs, Plus Spells and Witchy Rituals*. CICO Books, First published 2009.

Delicious Reference Websites for Further Explorations
Janewardwickecollings.com
Goddess-guide.com
Sydneymarkets.com.au
Witchipedia.com
Goddess-power.com

About the Author

I believe...
I believe food is the greatest love connection to self, loved ones, ancestry and Mother Earth.

I believe that when you're using your hands to select, prepare, cook and eat simple, seasonal foods, you're directly linking into your heart space, creating a love connection.

Love connection to self
When food is authentically aligned to self, based on personal life cycles and seasons, it becomes the greatest act of self-loving care you can gift to YOU.

Love connection to loved ones
When you share the foods you cook and create with your hands with others, you are literally sharing your love—an energetic imprint of you in every dish.

Love connection to ancestry
When you re-create food from your ancestry, you keep alive the food storytelling of your family and a deep soul connection to those who've passed.

Love connection to Mother Earth
When we eat the foods grown by Mother Earth, we are directly connecting to Her motherly love and energy. It's the greatest 'grounding' practice you will ever experience.

My magick...
My magick is my intuition and its ability to align food to your energetic desires so that you experience what authentic nourishment truly feels like—bliss!

My truth...
I am an expert in my field of food publishing and have been for more than 25 years with the cookbooks I have created and exposure I have received worldwide. I have co-created cookbooks with authors which have sold millions of dollars in copies worldwide over this time. I've self-published a cookbook and had the rights of cookbooks I've written for publishing companies sold in the USA and across Europe.

My food consulting business...
Has gifted me the opportunity to live and work here in Australia, the UK, the Middle East and Malaysia and receive prestigious awards from my industry peers.

Aside all of this though, I take deep gratitude in my passion, knowledge and attention to detail, all of which I am highly respected for in my industry.

While my career started in the world of food and lifestyle magazines (*BBC Good Food UK, Food & Travel UK, Jamie Oliver, Elle Cuisine, Australian Table, Gourmet Traveller, Donna Hay, Recipes +*), my true passion and the past decade have been focused on health cookbooks; with all published works focused on holistic living, food-specific health and wellbeing. I have produced work for all of Australia's leading health and wellness food personalities and advocates, with Michelle Bridges, Scott Gooding, Luke Hines, Dr

Libby, Dr Sue Shepherd, Pete Evans, Sarah Wilson and Julie Goodwin to name a few.

I'm professionally trained and accredited in food, cookery and recipe writing, as well as health coaching through IIN and life coaching with the Beautiful You Coaching Academy.

I can support you in bespoke 1:1 sessions or as part of a group collective experience. You can find out more at www.traceypattison.com

Food Index

apples, 182–3
    little lemon puddings, 208
    sweet baked apples with pastry top, 184
asparagus, 99–101
    quick roasted tart, 102
aubergine see eggplant
autumn seasoning, 160–1
avocados, 95
    attitudes towards, 60
    raw blueberry mousse, 152

baking, 107, 180
barbecuing, 140
barley
    sweet potatoes roasted with harissa barley, 202
beetroot, 209–11
    slow-roasted curry, 212
blanching, 131
blood oranges see oranges
blueberries, 150–1
    raw blueberry mousse, 150
braising, 131–2
breakfast, 20
broccoli, 172–4
    grilled, and quinoa salad, 175
broiling see grilling

cabbage, green, 176–8
    pan-fried cabbage and sage gnocchi, 179
cakes
    one-bowl blood orange teacake, 111
    slow-cooker sticky date choc cake, 221
celeriac, 195–7
    soup with dukkah flatbreads, 198
celery root see celeriac
celery seeds, in awakening salt, 94
chargrilling, stovetop, 116
chickpeas
    barbecued marinated eggplant and smashed hummus, 144
    slow-roasted beetroot curry, 212
chilli, in deep surrender salt, 190–1
cilantro see coriander
coconut aminos
    stri-fry ginger mushrooms with udon, 156
coconut cream
    raw blueberry mousse, 152
coconut sugar
    autumn seasoning, 160–1
    blanched peach with oolong tea syrup, 135
coconut, desiccated (shredded)
    little lemon puddings, 208
coriander, on slow-roasted beetroot curry, 212
crumble, stewed rhubarb, 215–17
curry, slow-roasted beetroot, 212
custard with preserved pears, 187

dates, 219–20
    slow-cooker sticky date choc cake, 221
deep surrender salt, 190–1
deep-frying, 214
desserts
    blanched peach with oolong tea syrup, 135
    chargrilled pineapple and mint limes, 120
    figs with saffron and toasted pistachio crumb, 167

little lemon puddings, 208
macerated mango and caramelised macadamia, 148
preserved pears, 187
raw blueberry mousse, 152
stewed rhubarb crumble, 218
sweet baked apples with pastry top, 184
vanilla simmered pink grapefruit, 106

dukkah
celeriac soup with dukkah flatbreads, 198

eggplant, 141–3
barbecued marinated eggplant and smashed hummus, 144

figs, 164–6
with saffron and toasted pistachio crumb, 167
frying, 116, 214

garbanzos see chickpeas
ginger
stir-fry ginger mushrooms with udon, 156
gnocchi
pan-fried cabbage and sage gnocchi, 179
grapefruit, pink, 103–5
vanilla simmered, 106
yoghurt with, 106
grilling, 171

harissa
sweet potatoes roasted with harissa barley, 202
hazelnuts, in asparagus tart, 102
hummus
barbecued marinated eggplant and smashed hummus, 144

ice cream see nice-cream

kumara see sweet potatoes

leeks, 168–9
with asparagus, 100
poached, with mustard dressing, 170
lemons, 205–7
little lemon puddings, 208
lentils, steamed peas and, 124
limes
with chargrilled pineapple, 120
macerated mango and caramelised macadamia, 148

macadamia, caramelised, and macerated mango, 148
macerating, 140
mango, 145–7
macerated, and caramelised macadamia, 148
mashing, 214
mealtimes, 20–1
measures, 228
mint, in summer seasoning, 128–9
mushrooms, 153–5
dried, 191
stir-fry ginger mushrooms with udon, 156

nice-cream
with little lemon puddings, 208
with sticky date choc cake, 221
with sweet baked apples, 184
noodles

stir-fry ginger mushrooms with udon, 156

oolong tea syrup, blanched peach with, 135
oranges, blood, 109–11
   one-bowl teacake, 111
oranges, in awakening salt, 94
oven temperatures, 228

pan-frying, 171
pasta, braised tomatoes for, 139
pastry
   quick roasted asparagus tart, 102
   sweet baked apples with pastry top, 184
peaches, 132–4
   blanched peach with oolong tea syrup, 135
pears, 185–6
   preserved, 187
peas, 121–3
   steamed, and lentil toss, 124
pineapple, 117–19
   chargrilled, and mint limes, 120
pistachios
   figs with saffron and toasted pistachio crumb, 167
plants-first philosophy, 18–19
poaching, 163
potatoes, new, 112–15
   sautéed with spring goddess dressing, 115
potatoes, sweet see sweet potatoes
preserving, 180
puddings, 203

quick roasting, 98
quinoa salad, grilled broccoli and, 175

raw foods, 149
rhubarb, 215–17
   crumble, 218
roasting, 98, 194, 203
rose petals, in autumn seasoning, 160–1

saffron
   in autumn seasoning, 160–1
   figs with saffron and toasted pistachio crumb, 167
sage gnocchi and pan-fried cabbage, 179
salt
   in awakening salt, 94
   in deep surrender salt, 190–1
sautéing, 108
seasonal food, 86–90
seasoning
   spring, 94–5
   summer, 128–9
   autumn, 160–1
   winter, 190–1
shallow frying, 116
simmering, 97
slow-cooker cooking, 213
slow-roasting, 203
soups, 194
   celeriac soup with dukkah flatbreads, 198
spaghetti, braised tomatoes for simple pasta, 139
spring seasoning, 94–5
steaming, 116
stewing, 213
stir-frying, 149
stovetop chargrilling, 116
strawberries
   in stewed rhubarb crumble, 215–17
summer seasoning, 128–9
sweet potatoes, 199–201
   roasted with harissa barley, 202

tart, asparagus, 102
tea, oolong
    blanched peach with oolong tea syrup, 135
temperatures, oven, 228
thyme, in awakening salt, 94
toasting, 163
tomatoes, 136–8
    braised, for simple pasta, 139

udon, stir-fry mushrooms with, 156

vanilla
    nice-cream, 184
    sugar, 129
    in summer seasoning, 128–9

weights and measures, 228
winter seasoning, 190–1

yoghurt
    with beetroot curry, 212
    with chargrilled pineapple, 120
    with pink grapefruit, 106
    with sticky date choc cake, 221
    with sweet baked apples, 184

www.ingramcontent.com/pod-product-compliance
Lightning Source LLC
Chambersburg PA
CBHW020319010526
44107CB00054B/1899